D0937256

THE QUEST
OF THE
CHRIST
OF FAITH

THE QUEST
OF THE
CHRIST
OF FAITH

**Reflections on
the Bultmann Era**

William Baird

Word Books, Publisher
Waco, Texas

First Printing–August 1977
Second Printing–February 1978

THE QUEST OF THE CHRIST OF FAITH

ISBN 0-8499-008-5
Library of Congress catalog card number: 77-075461

For Lisa and Eric

tékna phōtòs

Contents

Acknowledgements

The Bultmann era was an exciting time for biblical scholars. Though the era is over, it left a large legacy to those who were acquainted with its leaders. The opportunity for me to reflect on that legacy was made possible by a leave of absence spent at Heidelberg. The leave was granted by Texas Christian University's Brite Divinity School, and special appreciation is due to Chancellor James M. Moudy, (then) Vice-Chancellor James W. Newcomer, the late Dean Elmer Henson and Dean William E. Tucker (now president of Bethany College). A faculty fellowship grant from the American Association of Theological Schools provided additional support for the period of study abroad. At Heidelberg, my work was enriched by the hospitality of Prof. Günther Bornkamm, and my teacher of many years, Prof. Erich Dinkler.

Much of the material of this book was presented as New Testament lectures at the Northwest Preachers Parliament held at Northwest Christian College in January of 1973. I remain in debt to President Barton A. Dowdy, the faculty and student body of the college, together with the Disciple ministers of the northwest, for their kind reception. The lectures have been revised and expanded for publication.

Although this work hopes to make some contribution to the understanding of the Bultmann era, it is directed primarily to the general reader rather than the specialist. Consequently, an effort has been made to keep the notes to a minimum. Sources are cited only where direct references have been made. In the same way, the bibliography makes no attempt to be exhaustive. Sources are listed merely to indicate some representative works of the major figures discussed in the text. Bultmann is represented only by principal works available in English, and none of the many excellent interpretations of his theology have been included. Among the most useful are *The Thought of Rudolf Bultmann*, by André Malet, translated by Richard Strachan (Garden City, N.Y.: Doubleday, 1971), and *An Introduction to the Theology of Rudolf Bultmann*, by Walter Schmithals, translated by John Bowden (Minneapolis: Augsburg, 1968).

The manuscript was carefully read in various stages by my friend and colleague, Dean M. Jack Suggs. Though responsible for none of the book's shortcomings, his constructive criticism has been exceptionally helpful, not only here, but in all our work together over the last ten years. The book is dedicated to my children, Lisa and Eric, whose affection has lightened all my labors.

WILLIAM BAIRD

Chapter 1

Can This Be the Christ?

IN 1910, ALBERT SCHWEITZER's *Von Reimarus zu Wrede* (From Reimarus to Wrede) appeared in English translation as *The Quest of the Historical Jesus.* This title, an imaginative rendering of the original subtitle, may be more important than the book itself for dramatizing a major theological concern of the last two centuries: the search for the Jesus of history. Schweitzer's intention was to trace the history of the study of the life of Jesus from the work of Hermann Reimarus in the eighteenth century to the research of William Wrede in the twentieth. Yet, as Günther Bornkamm has pointed out, Schweitzer not only erected a monument to the quest, he also "delivered its funeral oration." [1] The participants in the quest had imagined that the modern tools of historical research could cut through the layers of church dogma to uncover the real Jesus, and that the Jesus who lived in history could become the pioneer and perfecter of faith for their day. In Schweitzer's opinion, however, this supposition that Jesus

11

ought to be relevant for man's faith had so dulled the tools of research that the historical Jesus remained buried under the debris of theological presuppositions. By way of contrast, the "Jesus" who emerged from the research was garbed in the clothing of nineteenth-century idealism, styled according to the pattern of Victorian virtues. Such a Jesus never existed, so that Schweitzer could conclude, "There is nothing more negative than the result of the critical study of the Life of Jesus." [2]

Schweitzer's own results were equally negative. Following the lead of Johannes Weiss, he pursued the historical Jesus along the path of consistent eschatology. From this perspective, Jesus appeared to be at home in the bizarre world of Jewish apocalyptic. He imagined that God was about to crash into history to destroy the cosmic order and set up a new heaven and a new earth. When the cataclysmic event did not occur as soon as he expected, Jesus rushed to Jerusalem to force God's hand, to upset the tables of the old order, to hurry to his tragic death that he might soon return in power, riding on the clouds as the supernatural Son of Man. In the self-confident culture of the dawning twentieth century, this Jesus had no place to lay his head. "The historical Jesus," says Schweitzer, "will be to our time a stranger and an enigma." [3]

Although his Jesus was really irrelevant, Schweitzer did not question the validity of the historical quest. He only supposed that his predecessors had not been sufficiently rigorous in the application of its method. That the search for the historical Jesus led up a blind alley remained for later scholars to discover. Actually, it is symbolic that Schweitzer's chronicle ends with William Wrede, since the latter's work did much to expose the problematic character of the quest. Whereas the earlier interpreters believed the Gospels were designed to present a picture of the life and teachings of Jesus, Wrede argued that the oldest and most reliable Gospel, the Gospel of Mark, was written to present a theology about Christ. The theme of this Gospel, the "messianic secret," presupposed belief that Jesus was the Messiah—a belief which, in Wrede's view, did not arise until after the resurrection. In attempting to project the messiahship back into Jesus' lifetime, Mark invented the "messianic secret"—a device which explained how Jesus, though truly the Messiah, was not recognized as such during his earthly career. The earliest Gospel, therefore, was not concerned with biography, but with theology. In order to uncover the Jesus of history beneath the layers of doctrine about Christ, the biblical historian would have to dig into strata of tradition older than the Gospel of Mark.

A method for probing this older tradition was soon developed. Borrowed from the Old Testament scholars and dubbed "form criticism," the new approach sought the historical Jesus by investigating reports about him which circulated before anything was written down. The investigation indicated, according to the form critics, that information about Jesus was handed down in tiny units: short stories or brief sayings. Although some of the material went back to Jesus himself, much of this tradition originated in the life of the church. The early Christians were not concerned to collect biographical data about Jesus, but to recount his deeds and words in order to proclaim him Lord and Christ. In the light of the resurrection faith, their memory of Jesus sitting on the hills of Galilee was illuminated by the vision of the Son of Man standing at the right hand of God. A biography of Jesus, because of the nature of our sources, could not be written; the quest of the historical Jesus appeared to be impossible.

According to James M. Robinson, the quest was not only impossible, it was theologically illegitimate.[4] Its primary assumption—that the Jesus discovered by historical research could be the ground of religious commitment—represented a false understanding of faith. For one thing, a faith like that depended on the shaky results of fallible biblical scholarship. Pity the poor man in the pew, who would have to hold his faith in suspension, waiting breathlessly for the latest archeological discovery from the Judean desert or the most recent theory about the authorship of Isaiah. Throughout its history, the church had produced a host of saints who had never heard of historical criticism. Moreover, the notion that faith had as its object the verified result of scientific research represented a faith which was no faith at all. Such a faith was actually belief in man's ability to prove, not faith in God whose ways were not our ways. Those who wanted to stand on some solid rock had failed to realize that faith involved a radical risk, that it was commitment to the crucified one, foolishness to philosophers and a scandal to historians.

If the quest for the historical Jesus had become both impossible and illegitimate, what new approach could be found to keep the enterprising biblical scholar occupied? The answer seems obvious: the quest of the Christ of faith. Actually, this new quest had been anticipated by two theologians in the latter part of the nineteenth century. Wilhelm Herrmann, a professor at Marburg who numbered among his students both Karl Barth and Rudolf Bultmann, proposed a new understanding of faith. In his view, faith was a matter of personal trust, experienced deep within the believer's existence. The object of faith was not biographical data about the man from Nazareth, but the inner life of Jesus—a life which could not be established by historical research, but which could be appropriated by religious experience. Martin Kähler, whose *The So-Called Historical Jesus and the Historic Biblical Christ* appeared ten years before Schweitzer's first edition, believed the liberal lives of Jesus to be sheer historical fabrication. He also considered Herrmann's "inner life of Jesus" to be totally beyond the purview of the historian—a psychological concoction created to read Ritchlian theology back into the Bible. All of these views, in Kähler's judgment, held the wrong object of faith. The concern of the church was not with the historical Jesus, but with the Christ of the Christian proclamation—what Kähler called "the Christ of the whole Bible." [5]

Although it may seem that these developments would have brought to an end the quest of the historical Jesus, lives of Jesus in the old mode and by the old method continued to be produced. Only a crisis in man's culture could sound the death-knell of the nineteenth-century search. The religion of the time was a cultural religion, involving a marriage of convenience between the Christian tradition and the virtues of contemporary society. When nineteenth-century culture collapsed in the tragedies of the twentieth century, nineteenth-century theology crumbled with it. The theological heralds of the new day looked back on the rubble with disdain. A religion created in man's image and built on the shifting sands of man's values could offer no sure ground for faith in the time of the shaking of the foundations. What man longed to hear was a word from God—a word beyond the feeble cry of the theologians and the paltry results of biblical research. It was to hear this word that Karl Barth began to study the Bible anew. For Barth, the word was no compendium of biblical texts, but the creative, redemptive Word of God made flesh in Jesus Christ. To this Word the Bible bore witness; to this Word the theologian must be captive. Karl Barth was calling for a biblical theology—a theology whose central concern was the quest of the Christ of faith.

Actually, Barth did not set out to contrast the Christ of faith with the historical Jesus, but to magnify God's historical revelation in Jesus Christ. The task of delineating the quest of the Christ of faith was left to Rudolf Bultmann. He had heard the stern call of Barth and left the flesh pots of nineteenth-century liberalism to follow. Yet, Bultmann kept one foot in Egypt, supposing that skills learned in the past might be useful in the trek toward the promised land. Bultmann was a theological synthesizer. His synthesis appropriated three factors which were primary concerns of the theology of the midtwentieth century: historical criticism, existentialist philosophy, and dialectical (or Barthian) theology. In taking up historical criticism, Bultmann was able to show that the old quest of the historical Jesus was impossible. In employing existentialism, he was able to argue that the old quest was illegitimate. In adopting dialectical theology, he was able to witness to the Christ of the biblical proclamation.

Bultmann's synthesis provided a theological framework wherein a host of biblical scholars could carry out their work. Although many did not adopt Bultmann's theological stance, most of the biblical theologians of the time built on some of the elements included in his structure. Practically all of them were committed to the historical method in biblical research, and many of them were sensitive to the existential element in biblical thought. Above all, the theologians of the era after World War II were responsive to the idea of God's revelation in Christ. While many of them considered this biblical Christ to be one with the Jesus of history, they were not content to relegate Jesus to the past. Their conviction that Jesus Christ was decisive for the life and thought of the church implied some understanding of a Christ of faith—a Christ who somehow transcended the temporal limitations of Jesus of Nazareth. No one, however, saw the implications of this issue as clearly as the man from Marburg. For Bultmann, the words of Paul were prophetic: "Even though we once knew Christ according to the flesh, we know him thus no longer" (2 Cor. 5:16, translation mine).

What of the present? Our time has been described as "the post-Bultmann era," or the time of the death of biblical theology.[6] The pupils of Bultmann are engaged in a new quest of the historical Jesus, and the old quest is being resumed with minor modifications. Some scholars are urging biblical studies to revert to the time before Barth, as though everything since had been an unfortunate theological nightmare. Biblical theology, we are told, should abandon its desire to be normative and restrict itself to the descriptive task, telling only what the Bible meant in its own time, and keeping silent about what it means today.[7] The resulting "crisis" in biblical theology,[8] raises the question of the proper role of the Bible in the whole theological drama. The centrality of the Scriptures, so basic to the Protestant heritage, has become problematic. The Scriptures, of course, gain their importance as witness to the Word of God revealed in Christ. Consequently, the problematic situation of the Bible creates a still more serious concern—the question concerning the essence of Christianity as a historical religion and the conviction that God has revealed himself in human history. For this question the biblical query is still relevant, "What think ye of Christ?" (Matt. 22:42, KJV).

The attempt to answer this question motivated the quest of the Christ of faith—the central concern of the Bultmann era. Although that era is gone, one may hope that an understanding of the immediate past may serve to clarify the issues of the current crisis. Just as Bultmann's synthesis can be depicted against the backdrop of the old quest, so an investigation of biblical theology's recent concern with the Christ of faith may bring into focus questions which confront the theologian of today. While it may be acknowledged that Bultmann's approach provided an itinerary which many could follow in the quest of the Christ of faith, the question remains whether the dissolution of the Bultmannian synthesis brings that quest to an end. In Robinson's terms we may ask: Is the quest of the Christ of faith possible and legitimate? The following study of the rise and fall of the Bultmann era is understood, therefore, as clearing the way for the important contemporary question: Is it possible and proper to pursue the quest for the Christ of faith in the post-Bultmannian period? In any event, historical Christianity finds it difficult to dispense with Jesus, and unless Jesus is to be relegated to the distant past—some shadowy figure in the memory of man's search for meaning—theology will continue to be concerned with the quest of the Christ of faith.

Chapter 2

Christ According to the Flesh

The Heritage of Historical Criticism

LIKE THE QUEST of the historical Jesus, the quest of the Christ of faith hailed the triumph of the historical critical method. This method, a major legacy of nineteenth-century liberalism, became one of the three main pillars supporting Bultmann's theological structure. By and large, historical criticism was an attempt to apply the procedures developed in the natural sciences to the study of historical sources. The method was empirical and rational, demanding careful collection and objective evaluation of the relevant data. Above all, historical criticism assumed that Christianity was a historical religion and that the best method of investigating history should be applied to the study of Christian origins. At first feared as a threat to religion, the historical critical method advanced in the nineteenth century and eventually was adopted by defenders of orthodoxy like J. Gresham Machen, in order to support such conservative conclusions as the historicity of the virgin birth.

Most of the practitioners of the historical method, however, were advocates of a liberal theology. Adolf Harnack, for example, believed the essence of Christianity could be discovered by employing "the methods of historical science." [1] Since science knew nothing of the divine interruption of the natural order, the miracle stories of the Gospels reflect the fantasies of a primitive world view rather than historical fact. Similarly, the resurrection was not to be understood in terms of the empty tomb or the Easter appearances, but as a sign of a timeless truth: life is eternal. This sort of truth could be found, according to Harnack, when historical method was used to distinguish between the husk and kernel in the preaching of Jesus. When the husk was stripped away, the essence of Christianity shone forth—the Fatherhood of God and the infinite worth of the human soul. For all the variety of its historical forms, Christianity had a permanent validity which came to expression in Jesus' command of love. With Harnack, historical criticism was enlisted in the service of a liberal theology which found the essence of Christianity in the teachings of the historical Jesus.

The History of Religions

Early in the twentieth century two currents were to arise within historical criticism which would inundate the historical foundations of liberal theology: the *religionsgeschichtliche Schule* and form criticism. The former, usually translated the "history of religions school," simply took seriously the basic intention of the historical method to understand the early Christian sources in their original setting. To accomplish this goal, the members of the school engaged in a thorough study of the religions of the Graeco-Roman world. They pursued this research, however, with a new vigor. Previous interpretation of the Bible, they believed, had been moved by doctrinal and utilitarian interests. As a result, the Bible had been viewed as a repository of doctrine, and used as catechetical manual for modern Christians. Instead, the New Testament should be understood as witness to the faith of vital people who lived in another time and breathed the air of a different culture.

The History of Religions School

Nineteenth-century forerunners of the modern movement were already convinced that early Christianity was the syncretistic product of Jewish and Hellenistic forces. At the dawn of the new century, however, light was thrown on the study of Jesus from the perspective of consistent eschatology—a view developed by Johannes Weiss and made popular by Albert Schweitzer. Weiss believed the central feature of the teachings of Jesus to be his proclamation of the kingdom of God. The message of the kingdom, however, was no calm communication of ethical truths, but the shattering announcement of an eschatological event. Like the apocalyptic prophets of his time, Jesus was convinced that the end of the world was at hand, the ax already at the root of the tree. God was about to break into history in a cataclysmic manner; the coming of his kingdom was to be a supernatural happening of the imminent future. As a result of Weiss's work, the major element in the teachings of Jesus was seen to be mistaken in its reading of the signs of the times—a fantastic dream about a future which never came. The Jesus of Johannes Weiss bore almost no resemblance at all to the portrait by Adolf Harnack.

Whereas Weiss portrayed Jesus against the backdrop of apocalyptic Judaism, the main representatives of the history

of religions school depicted early Christianity in the bright
colors of Hellenistic religion. An attempt to trace the origin
of this wide-spread Hellenistic syncretism was made by Richard Reitzenstein. According to Reitzenstein, the Graeco-
Roman religions of redemption echoed an ancient myth concerning the origin and destiny of man which found its ultimate
source in Iranian religion. This myth's vision of a primal Man
from which the souls of all men were derived is reflected in
the early Christian confession of the Son of Man. Its anthropological dualism—the notion that man was composed of
divine spirit and evil body—is assumed in Paul's description
of the warfare between the spirit and the flesh. Indeed, Paul
was himself a Gnostic who understood Christ in terms of the
myth of the Redeemer, the heavenly Man who descended to
earth in order to lead the souls of the redeemed back to the
higher realms from which they came. The message which Paul
proclaimed was merely another form of the universal religion
of redemption.

The significance of the history of religions method for New
Testament research is more fully revealed in the work of
Wilhelm Bousset. Like Reitzenstein, Bousset observed that the
accouterments of Hellenistic religion were acquired when
the church moved from Palestine to the gentile world. Bousset
viewed the Hellenistic church as the bridge between Palestinian Christianity and the religion of Paul. Within the Hellenistic church, the shift to the new shape of faith was
signaled by the use of the title *Kyrios*, or "Lord," for Jesus.
This title was widely employed in the Graeco-Roman world
to honor the deities of the Hellenistic cults. When applied to
Jesus, the title indicated that he had been assigned the role
of deity, and as Christ had become the object of the church's
worship. For Paul, this change took the form of a Christ-

mysticism or cult-mysticism, wherein the presence of Christ as Lord of the cultic life of the community was attested by the gifts of the Spirit. The religion of the Fourth Gospel, however, was even farther removed from the Palestinian faith. Here Christ-mysticism had been succeeded by a God-mysticism in which man could become divine through the vision of the deity. In second-century Gnosticism the Hellenization of Christianity was complete. "If Paul has already woven a redemption myth around the historical figure of Jesus of Nazareth, here now the historical is altogether swallowed up by the myth." [2]

Bousset's own faith was unshaken by these results. For him, as for Harnack, the essence of Christianity was to be found in Jesus. His picture of the man from Nazareth is painted in hues borrowed from the palette of nineteenth-century liberalism. "And among all these teachers favored by God, who have forced open the heavens for us and called down the fire of faith, stands the figure of Jesus of Nazareth, towering high above all others, as all eyes can see." [3] Jesus, as Weiss had pointed out, was mistaken about the time of the coming of the kingdom, yet his teaching embodied eternal truth: the idea of God as personal and spiritual, the Father of every human individual. In short, Bousset employed the history of religions method to support his notion of the uniqueness and relevance of Jesus. Had he applied the method with equal rigor to the study of the Synoptic Gospels, Bousset might have discovered a Jesus as strange as his picture of the early Christian cult—a man nobody knows or even wants to know.

The History of Religions and Rudolf Bultmann

In his quest for the Christ of faith, Rudolf Bultmann has

been a student of the history of religions school. His criticism
of nineteenth-century liberalism has focused on its failure to
acknowledge the implications of the *religionsgeschichtliche
Methode* for the study of Christian origins. "Harnack," he
said, "never caught a glimpse of the utter strangeness of the
image of primitive Christianity disclosed by the religious-
historical school." [4]

Bultmann's own use of the method is illustrated by his
distinctive presentation of the historical heritage of early
Christianity. His interpretation is presented in a stereotyped
pattern which moves from good to bad and back to good—
from the Old Testament to Judaism and back to Jesus. The
original and valid understanding of man and the world is
found in the Old Testament. In stark contrast to the Greek
view of man as a part of the cosmos, the Hebrews saw man
as a creation of God. This God of the Old Testament is the
mighty God who acts in history to accomplish his purposes.
Through his potent Word he makes himself known, and
through obedience to this Word man can accept his authentic
being as responsible to the Creator. Since God's purposes and
man's obedience are never complete in the present, God's
action is always directed toward a future fulfillment. The
possibility of authentic existence, however, continues to confront man in the present as he responds to the call for
obedience to God's purposes.

These valid ideas are eroded in Judaism and ignored in
Hellenism. For the former, the action of God was relegated to
the distant past. In the past God had given his law to man.
Getting right with God, therefore, required obedience to the
letter of the ancient code, while recompense was postponed to
a suprahistorical future. The God who acted in the present in
order to fulfill his goals for history was largely forgotten, and

the man who once responded to the acts of the Creator in order to receive his true being became preoccupied with his own efforts to attain legalistic salvation. In Hellenism, on the other hand, the problem of man was construed metaphysically. Although man had his origin from the higher powers, his life had become entrapped in an evil world. This imprisonment, however, was not the result of human responsibility, but of a cosmic fate over which man had no control. Man could only break the bonds of this metaphysical determinism by a flight from the world—a flight patterned after the ascent of the unhistorical hero of the Gnostic redemption myth.

With Jesus there is a return to the more valid understanding of God and man which Bultmann had discovered in the Old Testament. Jesus revived a vital concern for the action of God in the present through his sharp attack on Jewish legalism and his dramatic announcement of the imminent reign of God. In contrast to the apocalyptic seers whose imagery he employed, Jesus did not push this action into the distant future, but detected the finger of God already casting out demons in the present. God "meets man not only in the future judgment, but already here and now in daily life, with its challenges and opportunities." [5] In the present, man is called to decision in response to the God whose reign is about to be realized in history.

According to Bultmann, this "correct" understanding of man before God is refined by Paul and John. Paul, while continuing to use apocalyptic imagery, has deapocalypticized eschatology in his conviction that the decisive eschatological event has occurred in the death-resurrection of Christ. Although Christ is depicted in the image of the Gnostic Redeemer, the proclamation of Christ is understood as an eschatological event—an event in which God acts to call man to decision and faith. The Fourth Gospel, while presenting the Redeemer in the garb of the Hellenistic *logos*, declares that the Word became flesh and enacted the deeds of redemption on the stage of history. In John, the distracting·remnant of an apocalyptic future is removed entirely, so that God's present action in the Word is given its proper preeminence.

Bultmann, like Bousset, has used the history of religions method to distinguish the essential in Christianity from the unessential. Yet, whereas Bousset discerns the essential in the religion and ethics of the historical Jesus, Bultmann has discovered it in the Word of God—the Word spoken by the prophets, made flesh in Jesus, proclaimed by the apostles. Since "the only content of the Word of God is *Christ*," [6] the Christ who calls men to the decision of faith, the major impetus of Bultmann's biblical theology is the quest for the Christ of faith.

The Triumph of the History of Religions

Although the shocking conclusions of the *religionsge-schichtliche Schule* were often shunned, its method has been employed by almost all recent interpreters of the New Testament. The adoption of the method was encouraged by the discovery of new material such as the Dead Sea Scrolls and the Nag Hammadi texts. Actually, the attempt to interpret Christianity in the context of Hellenistic culture was not new to Britain and America. Edwin Hatch had looked at the relationship of Greek philosophy and Christianity in his Hibbert Lectures of 1889 *(The Influence of Greek Ideas on Christianity)*, and this tradition was carried on by such capable Hellenistic scholars as A. D. Nock and E. R. Goodenough.

Parallels can also be observed between the history of

religions movement and the Chicago school of the early twentieth century. Shirley Jackson Case, its most instructive representative, displayed familiarity with the works of Reitzenstein and Bousset as early as 1914. With the history of religions school, Case agreed that the church's transplant from Jewish to gentile soil involved a major transformation of early Christianity wherein Paul preached "the new gospel in the form of a mystery," and "John presented the new religion in the form of a 'gnosis.' " [7] Case's own approach stressed the evolutionary character of the early Christian movement. Previous study, he believed, had been moved by dogmatic interests, and even the liberal attempt to discover some abiding essence had distorted the understanding of Christian origins. In contrast to the search for normative doctrine, Case interpreted the ongoing life of the early Christianity as a developing social movement. His intent was not to study the New Testament as a collection of theological documents but "to place stress upon the Christian society out of which this literature came." [8] Thus, Case not only approved the history of religions approach, he anticipated its significance for the development of form criticism.

Not all responses to the history of religions school were positive. While acknowledging that Paul was at home in a Hellenistic environment, H. A. A. Kennedy argued that the apostle's thought was founded on the Old Testament and shaped with little resemblance to the patterns of the Graeco-Roman mystery cults. An explicit response to the *religionsgeschichtliche Schule* was undertaken by Carl Kraeling, a student of E. F. Scott. Kraeling's *Anthropos and Son of Man* (1927) was a thoroughly documented analysis of Reitzenstein's basic thesis. While recognizing that speculation about the primal Man was pre-Christian and Iranian in origin,

Kraeling argued that the soteriological aspect of the redemption myth was relatively late. In regard to Iranian influence on the New Testament image of the Son of Man, Kraeling concluded, "The elements included in the Mesopotamian phase of proto-Gnostic thought, were, so far as we have analyzed them, of no direct importance for the growth of Christian convictions." [9] A short time later, F. C. Burkitt argued that Gnosticism could have exercised no influence on earliest Christianity, since it was itself the product of second-century Christianity's attempt to cope with the problem of the delay of the eschaton.

During the Bultmann era, the history of religions method made its mark on biblical theologians who represent viewpoints at variance with the man from Marburg. C. H. Dodd, for example, interprets the Gospel of John within its contemporary setting, giving careful attention to Gnosticism and the Hermetic literature. To be sure, Dodd believes Old Testament and rabbinic backgrounds to be important in the exegesis of the Fourth Gospel, yet the imagery of John reflects a Jewish-Hellenistic syncretism like that displayed in Philo. Moreover, Dodd's famous "realized eschatology," though attributed to Jesus, finds its clearest expression in the Fourth Gospel. Thus a view of the end couched in the language of Hellenistic Judaism is decisive for Dodd's own formulation of the Christian faith.

The sensitivity to Jewish backgrounds is still more apparent in the works of Dodd's disciple, W. D. Davies. While acknowledging that Paul was influenced by Hellenistic factors, Davies argues that major elements in his thought can be explained in terms of rabbinic religion. The concept of the first and second Adam, for example, is not the fruit of an Iranian myth, but is rooted in the rabbinic idea of the unity of mankind in Adam. Davies, of course, recognizes that Hellenistic concepts have invaded Jewish thought via Hellenistic Judaism as illustrated by Philo and the Wisdom literature. This kind of backdrop sets the stage for Davies's most distinctive biblical interpretation: Paul identifies Christ as the new Torah, as the new revelation of God's law. Within Hellenistic Judaism, the Torah had been associated with Wisdom, the divine mediator and instrument of creation. Paul, picking up this identification, presents Christ as the new Torah-Wisdom, and thus, the preexistent agent of creation and redemption. The result is a Christology which owes nothing to the Gnostic redeemer myth and everything to rabbinic Wisdom speculation. In spite of his preference for Jewish backgrounds, Davies, like most other New Testament scholars of the midtwentieth century, heralds the triumph of the history of religions method.

Form Criticism

Building on the results of the history of religions method, a second methodological procedure of significance for twentieth-century biblical research is form criticism. *Formgeschichte*, as it was originally called, is a method whereby the development of oral traditions is analyzed. Applied to the New Testament, it has been primarily concerned with the tradition about Jesus, and consequently has focused its major attention on the Synoptic Gospels. An attempt to study the oral tradition behind the narratives of the Old Testament had already been made by Hermann Gunkel, one of Bultmann's teachers at Berlin. Gunkel, who had been active in the history of religions school, had tried to discern the life situations which shaped the stories about the Hebrew patriarchs. Form criticism was also encouraged by the belief that the Gospels were not classical treatises, but folk literature. In their essential character, these documents preserved the form of expression of folk tradition—a mode of expression found in the sagas and stories of ancient peoples.

The application of the form critical method to the gospel material was instigated by three scholars working independently: K. L. Schmidt, Martin Dibelius, and Rudolf Bultmann. Schmidt, whose *Der Rahmen der Geschichte Jesu* appeared in 1919, argued that the framework of the gospel narrative was largely an editorial fabrication. As such, it had little historical or biographical significance. Dibelius believed the oral tradition which the editor-evangelists used had been shaped by the needs of the expanding church. As the missionaries of the new faith went forth to proclaim their message, they had to declare who Jesus was, what he said, and what he did. Thus, the stories about Jesus and the reports of his teachings were illustrations for early Christian sermons. "Whatever was told of Jesus' words and deeds," wrote Dibelius, "was always a testimony of faith as formulated for preaching and exhortation in order to convert unbelievers and confirm the faithful." [10]

Rudolf Bultmann and Form Criticism

Bultmann's use of form criticism is more comprehensive and more radical. Commenting on his *History of the Synoptic Tradition* (1921), Burton Scott Easton, an American scholar largely sympathetic with *Formgeschichte*, has written that "Bultmann appears as the most radical serious critic since the days of Strauss." [11] In developing the method, Bultmann builds on assumptions which are basic to form critical work. The primary intent of form criticism is to detect the Jesus of history. Thus the goal of the method is, in Bultmann's own words, "the attainment of the most accurate possible picture of the life and teaching of the historical Jesus." [12] Like the other form critics, Bultmann believes oral tradition about Jesus circulated in small, isolated units. These units, or forms, had been shaped by the interests of the church—interests which were not only evangelistic (Dibelius), but also polemic, apologetic, catechetic, and cultic. With Schmidt, Bultmann agrees that the gospel narrative is a mosaic of tiny bits of tradition worked into a vague design by the authors of the Gospels.

Major effort is expended by the form critics in the search to discern the *Sitz-im-Leben* or "life situation" in which the various elements of the developing tradition find their origin. What elements go back to Jesus? What elements have been inserted by the church? How has the tradition been shaped in the process of transmission? In answering these questions, Bultmann makes much of the *religionsgeschichtliche* distinction between the Palestinian and the Hellenistic church. If some feature of the tradition bears the marks of the mystery cults, for example, this aspect of the tradition cannot be traced back to Jesus but must be located in the later situation of the gentile church. Bultmann also supposes that the way Matthew and Luke use the tradition they have received suggests how tradition is formulated generally in the ongoing life of the Christian community. In his attempt to identify the life situations of the gospel tradition, Bultmann likewise has utilized fascinating parallels which he has detected in extrabiblical sources. For example, Jewish and Hellenistic stories about heroes and healers also circulated by word of mouth. A study of these parallels indicates that universal principles operate whenever oral tradition is transmitted—principles whereby the tradition about Jesus can be analyzed and evaluated.

In analyzing the tradition about Jesus, Bultmann divides the material into narratives and teachings. The latter, in turn, are classified as either apothegms or dominical sayings. An apothegm (or paradigm, according to Dibelius) is a brief story which provides the setting for an important pronouncement (e.g., Mark 2:23–28). While many sayings of this sort represent authentic words of Jesus, such stories are usually the product of the Palestinian church. They find parallels in the rabbinic sources and betray a tendency on the part of the developing tradition to depict Jesus in the role of a respected rabbi. The dominical sayings—sayings of the Lord—are further classified into smaller categories. Most important of these are the prophetic and apocalyptic pronouncements, for example the beatitudes and woes in Luke 6:20–26. Such teachings characterize Jesus' primary mission of proclaiming the kingdom and demanding repentance. Rather than reveling in apocalyptic speculation, the words of Jesus share the vigor and originality of the ancient prophets. "In these utterances," writes Bultmann, "it is possible to detect with some probability genuine words of Jesus, for there can be no doubt that Jesus appeared as prophet and announcer of the coming Kingdom of God." [13]

In analyzing the narrative tradition, Bultmann arranges the material into two main categories: miracle stories and historical stories or legends. The former, which include the nature miracles as well as healings, are viewed with skepticism. "On the basis, then, of the similarity between the miracles stories in the synoptic gospels and those in Hellenistic literature we are forced to conclude that these miracle stories do not belong to the oldest strata of tradition, but, at least in their present form, were elaborated in Hellenistic Christianity." [14] A similar skepticism permeates Bultmann's treatment of the historical stories. The confession of Peter, for example, is a legend smuggled into the account to allege that Jesus was recognized as Messiah during his earthly career. Even the passion story, which some form critics believed to be the earliest collection of narrative material, was composed of legendary elements and designed for dogmatic purposes. The portrait which survives this critical onslaught depicts Jesus as an eschatological prophet who attacks Jewish legalism and heralds the kingdom of God.

The Advance of Form Criticism

Regardless of Bultmann's conclusions, the form critical method has been widely appropriated. To be sure, the earliest responses were sharply critical. It was observed, for example, that the form critics had overestimated the significance of the oral period. The time between the events of the life of Jesus and the writing of the Gospel of Mark was relatively short, so that forces which operated in the transmission of ancient folklore could scarely be expected to function. Indeed, the gap was so narrow that the evangelists could have used reports which were not far removed from the eyewitnesses. "If the Form-Critics are right," quipped one critic, "the disciples must have been translated into heaven immediately after the Resurrection." [15] Moreover, it seemed strange that the form critical school attributed so little originality to Jesus, the founder of the faith, and so much to the community of his followers. Evidence of the subjectivity of the form critics was apparent in the disparity of their varying classifications of the traditional material and in their notion that the early Christians had no real interest in history and biography. A more serious criticism, however, was voiced by Erich Fascher, one of the first scholars to take form criticism seriously. Already by 1924, Fascher observed that the advocates of *Formgeschichte* sometimes confused analysis of tradition with evaluation of history. As far as method was concerned, the critics were restricted to the classification of forms, but they sometimes wandered beyond the analysis of forms into conclusions about historical authenticity. "The form alone," wrote Fascher, "allows no historical value-judgments." [16]

Actually, it was this distinction between method and evaluation which facilitated the extensive use of form criticism. In his lectures *The Gospel before the Gospels* (1928), Burton Scott Easton introduced form criticism to an American audience. Easton recognized the importance of the oral tradition and employed the categories of the form critics in his interpretation of the Synoptics. With Fascher, however, he shared doubts about form critical conclusions and insisted that form criticism be used merely as a method. "By itself," he wrote, "it can tell us nothing of the truth or falsity of events narrated." [17] Nevertheless, Easton thought the method could throw light on the earliest tradition and considered this "reason enough to give the new discipline our full attention." [18] Still more enthusiastic was F. C. Grant who believed that whenever transmission of tradition was involved in historical research, something like form criticism was a virtual necessity.

Form criticism was given sympathetic appraisal by two British scholars, Vincent Taylor and R. H. Lightfoot. Writing in 1933, Taylor accepted the basic assumption that the gospel tradition first circulated in small, isolated units. He also used the form critical method, with modifications, in his own synoptic research, redesignating, for example, the apothegms as "pronouncement-stories"—a designation which has become increasingly popular. The classification of some material as "legend," however, he eschewed, since it involved moving beyond the form critical method into the arena of historical evaluation. When form criticism was confined to its proper function, it could be a useful tool for the reconstruction of the life of Jesus. Lightfoot, while less confident about historical results, was convinced of the validity of the form critical approach. He not only adopted the method, he agreed that the apothegms were primary and the miracle stories secondary, and argued that the gospel narrative was largely unreliable because the early church had little interest in an accurate historical record of the life of Jesus.

Although this conclusion was offensive to many, the form critical method became increasingly popular. More than thirty years after Taylor and Lightfoot, W. D. Davies could observe, "It should be recognized that all serious students of the New Testament today are to some extent Form Critics"— words cited with approval in a recent New Testament introduction written by the conservative theologians Glenn W. Barker, William L. Lane, and J. Ramsey Michaels.[19] Other scholars antithetic to Bultmann have espoused the form critical method. Joachim Jeremias, for instance, has employed it as a primary technique in his monumental study of the parables and in his ardent quest for the *ipsissima verba Jesu*. Rather than accepting the conclusions of Bultmann and Lightfoot, Jeremias has adopted the form critical approach as a neutral method appropriate for the reconstruction of the historical Jesus. Nevertheless, it seemed apparent that the material left for the reconstruction had been reduced to a residual minimum. If the earliest tradition circulated in small units which had parallels in Jewish and Hellenistic folklore, and if the tradition had been molded to meet the needs of the developing Christian community, and if the Gospels were primarily confessional rather than historical documents, then it was evident that the quest of the historical Jesus had become increasingly problematic. Many found it difficult to resist the earlier conclusion of Lightfoot: "It seems, then, that the form of the earthly no less than of the heavenly Christ is for the most part hidden from us. For all the inestimable value of the gospels, they yield us little more than a whisper of his voice; we trace in them but the outskirts of his ways." [20]

Historical Criticism and the Christ of Faith

Historical criticism, comprising the triumph of the history of religions method and the advance of form criticism, left the biblical theology of the midtwentieth century with a large legacy. While this legacy devalued the quest of the historical Jesus, it provided capital in support of the quest of the Christ of faith. The earlier quest had assumed that Jesus was the proper object of faith, that he represented a unique phenomenon within the history of religion, and that his life and teachings were somehow normative for modern Christianity. The history of religions school, however, taught the theologian that Christianity was originally an amalgam of Graeco-Roman religions, not unique, but composed of elements mined in Jewish apocalyptic and Hellenistic Gnosticism. Therefore it was not appropriate for modern man, but belonged to another economy.

To be sure, the problem was reduced when the background of early Christianity was traced not to paganism but to the

Old Testament and Judaism. The work of Davies, for example, could provide some shelter for those caught in the cold blast of the *religionsgeschichtliche* method. If the primary source of early Christianity could be located in Israel, then the Old Testament could be appropriated as the book of the acts of God which culminated in Jesus Christ. Nevertheless, the Christ re-created by the history of religions method was to the twentieth century an alien from a foreign land. The liberal Jesus of Bousset was overcome by the apocalyptic prophet of Johannes Weiss. In the modern world, this Jesus had no place to call his home. Similarly, the attempt of Paul to move the apocalyptic teacher out of the Jewish ghetto into the wide world of Hellenism did not succeed in bringing Christ into the experience of modern man. The habitation constructed on Hellenistic soil was built according to a pagan blueprint—a structure made from cosmic materials and designed to accommodate a mythological redeemer. Even Davies's image of a Pauline Christ garbed in rabbinic Wisdom speculation looked out of place on the sidewalks of New York. Like the historical Jesus, the Christ of New Testament Christology seemed to be an illusive phantom, shrouded in the dark mists of a distant culture.

The results of form criticism were no less disappointing. Designed to equip scholarship in the quest of the historical Jesus, *Formgeschichte* demonstrated that the old quest led into a dead-end street. The Gospels in their present form were shown to be unreliable sources for the reconstructing of the life and teachings of Jesus. Not only did the evangelists lack biographical interest, they portrayed Jesus in their own theological image. Moreover, the attempt to go behind these confessional documents to an authentic historical tradition proved equally frustrating. The oral tradition was shaped to the church's needs, and its earliest units betray a dearth of interest in historical detail. Indeed, the first witnesses to Jesus, including the eyewitnesses of his life and death, were not concerned with biographical details but with theology: how the crucified one had become Lord and Christ. The quest for the historical Jesus had stripped away one layer of tradition after another, only to discover each time another layer. Somewhere beneath the tradition, of course, was the man from Nazareth, but this Jesus had been buried under the debris of the church's doctrine. Many who viewed the void created by form criticism shared the despair of Mary Magdalene, "They have taken away my Lord, and I do not know where they have laid him" (John 20:13).

Search parties were hastily organized. Scandinavian scholars like Harald Riesenfeld and Birger Gerhardsson argued that Jesus had used a rabbinic method in the instruction of his disciples—a method requiring verbal memorization. Consequently, the gospel tradition which had its source in Jesus himself had been transmitted with minimal modification. On the other hand, F. C. Grant, one of the early advocates of form criticism, seemed oblivious to its dangers. "Form criticism," he wrote, "gives us a renewed sense of the greatness, and the essential trustworthiness, of the earliest evangelical tradition, 'the living and abiding voice' of one who 'spake as never man spake' and yet spake 'as man.'" [21] Similarly, E. F. Scott, in his book *The Validity of the Gospel Record*, held that since the forms took definite shape early and there was evidence that the tradition had been preserved by a mutually corrective community, form criticism confirmed rather than denied the gospel record. Although their position was not without strength, these defenders of the faith failed to observe that the intention of their quest was quite different from the concern of the Gospels. Whereas the Gospels were dedicated to proclaiming the Christ of the church's faith, the scholars were committed to reconstructing the historical Jesus—the Jesus who could provide sure ground for the faith of modern man. The results, rather than being faithful to the gospel tradition, reflected the interests of nineteenth-century historicism. The Jesus of the historical quest was the creation of modern historical research.

No biblical theologian at midtwentieth century treasured the heritage of historical criticism more than Rudolf Bultmann. A participant in the work of the history of religions school, he also pioneered in the method of form criticism. Moreover, Bultmann recognizes the skepticism implicit in historical critical results and radicalizes it. He believes the gospel record to be historically unreliable and the quest of the historical Jesus to be virtually impossible. "I do indeed think," says Bultmann, "that we can now know almost nothing concerning the life and personality of Jesus." [22] This much misunderstood quotation should not be taken to mean that Bultmann denies all knowledge of the historical Jesus. What cannot be known is the inner life, the heroic struggle, which so fascinated the earlier interpreters. The trouble with the old quest was its attempt to go beyond what the sources provided. Careful historical method could show that Jesus was a Galilean prophet, that he associated with John the Baptist, that his major role was proclaiming the kingdom, that he was executed by the Romans. This Jesus, though at home in first-century Palestine, was utterly out of place in the modern world—his view of the end of the world was depicted in the fantastic images of Jewish apocalyptic, his notion of the time of God's cataclysmic act was totally mistaken.

Bultmann, however, has taken up the sword of historical

criticism and beaten it into a plowshare. The very weapon which could destroy the quest of the historical Jesus could prepare the ground for the quest of the Christ of faith. Just as form criticism showed that the old quest was impossible, and the history of religions method demonstrated that its object was irrelevant, so Bultmann could declare that the Jesus of historical reconstruction was not the proper basis for faith. This Jesus was the product of human research and as such participated in the frailties of humanity. Besides, this Jesus is not the object of the biblical faith. As Martin Kähler had already pointed out in 1896, the early Christians were concerned not with the Jesus of historical construction, but with the living Christ of the church's proclamation. Form criticism had been shown to be more "biblical" than liberalism, since it put the emphasis where the New Testament had originally placed it—on the confession of the community of faith.

Failure to acknowledge the essential character of the proclamation of the early church proved to be a stumbling block to the leaders of the history of religions school. "Like the liberals," accused Bultmann, "they are silent about a decisive act of God in Christ proclaimed as the event of redemption." [23] While Bultmann agreed with the *religionsgeschichtliche* estimate of Jesus as an apocalyptic prophet, and acknowledged the mythological character of early christological formulation, he insisted that the faith of the early Christians was unique in its own time and normative for ours.

Bultmann was not insensitive to the question of why Christianity, rather than other Hellenistic faiths, survived if it were merely an instance of Hellenistic syncretism. In response, he, like some members of the history of religions school, attempted to discern what was essential within the original expression of the Christian faith. Rather than looking to the personality of Jesus (which remained obscure) or the teachings of Jesus (which were paralleled in Jewish apocalyptic literature), Bultmann tuned his ear to the Word of God—the transcendent power working through the words of Jesus. As historical research indicates, Jesus is an eschatological prophet who proclaims the will of God and calls men to obedience, the "bearer of the word." [24] This understanding of Jesus also provides the clue for detecting a continuity between what was essential in Jesus and what was essential in the faith of the earliest Christians—the kerygma, the Word of God. This proclamation is itself a dynamic event which cannot be equated with the sermons of the apostles nor subject to the scrutiny of the historians. All efforts to absolutize or perpetuate the ancient formulae represent preoccupation with myth, not gospel. Beneath the forms of the Gospels, and the formulations of the Epistles, however, is a valid understanding of human existence—an understanding hidden in the inner chamber of the biblical message but open to those initiated into the mysteries of existentialist philosophy.

Chapter 3

Christ for Us

The Perspective of Existentialism

ACCORDING TO A distinguished philosopher of religion, "It is not possible to understand the inner development of Protestant theology during the past thirty years without confronting existential philosophy and its basic ideas." [1] If we are to comprehend the Bultmannian quest of the Christ of faith, we will have to come to grips with the question: What is existentialism?

Sired by the Danish prophet Sören Kierkegaard (1813–55), existentialist philosophy is a protest against traditional metaphysics and rationalism. The search for the essence of reality, according to Kierkegaard, had been lost in the maze of the Hegelian system and diverted into a pursuit of the nature of things. The more important question of the meaning of human existence could be answered not by objective inquiry but only by the subject who exists. Philosophy must turn its eye inward. Above all, philosophy must become passionately concerned with the existence of man—a being fraught with ambiguity and trapped in despair. Escape from this bondage could be attained only by a leap of faith. No exercise of reason could prepare for this leap, since it is utterly absurd—a leap into the dark. The object of this risky faith is no objective absolute built on metaphysical rock and buttressed by theological argument, but the God who transcends the world of finitude and temporality. Yet, man can have faith in this God since he has come into history in the form of the God-man, Jesus Christ.

More important for Bultmann's theology is the early work of the twentieth-century German philosopher Martin Heidegger. Although reluctant to be classified as an existentialist, Heidegger insists that fundamental philosophical questions "can only be put in such a way that the questioner as such is by his very questioning involved in the questions." [2] History, for example, is not an objective chronicle of events, but reflects the decision of man, who participates in history. In brief, Heidegger's complex system involves a phenomenological analysis of *Dasein*, which literally means "being there" and is Heidegger's term for human existence. The function of philosophy is to observe and analyze the phenomenon of human being. *Dasein* cannot be explained on the basis of some prior metaphysical theory but must be described simply as being there in the world. In the world, human being has the possibility of either authentic or inauthentic existence. In inauthentic existence, man is caught in the morass of things, preoccupied with externals, ensnared in the concerns of the world. Authentic existence, on the other hand, is attained by man's decision. Prompted by conscience, man becomes anxious about his own finitude or nonbeing. Authenticity is achieved when he acknowledges that he is a being destined for death. When he embraces this tragic threat of nonbeing and accepts himself in his radical finitude, man has achieved his true authenticity—a freedom from a false understanding of himself.

Existential Elements in Bultmann's Theology

The significance of existentialism for the theology of Rudolf Bultmann is widely recognized. Bultmann himself admits that existentialist philosophy is of "decisive significance" [3] for him. In the spirit of Kierkegaard, Bultmann insists that truth can be perceived only by the risk of faith. It is Heidegger's brand of existentialism, however, which has made its mark on Bultmann—an influence which can be traced to their mutual association at the University of Marburg. During Heidegger's tenure there (1922–28), a close relationship developed between philosopher and theologian. Bultmann participated in Heidegger's seminar on the philosophy of history and Heidegger took part in Bultmann's seminar on the theology of Paul. For our purposes, a sketch of three areas will suffice to illustrate the importance of existentialism for Bultmann's quest of the Christ of faith: the problem of understanding, the doctrine of man, and the idea of history.

The Problem of Understanding

For Bultmann, understanding does not mean the collection and arrangement of intellectual data; it means self-understanding. Self-understanding, in turn, is not some sort of psychological introspection, but man coming to grips with his own existence. For Bultmann, self-understanding is parallel to Heidegger's idea of the understanding of *Dasein*. It has two main aspects: First, the understanding of the being of man, that is, the philosophical analysis of the structure of human existence, or what Bultmann calls ontological or *existential* understanding; second, the understanding of a particular man in his specific situation, or what Bultmann calls ontic or *existentiell* understanding. Like Heidegger, Bultmann sees man in search of an authentic understanding of his existence—an understanding which rests on adequate philosophical analysis and speaks effectively to man's concrete condition.

According to Bultmann, man can attain an authentic understanding of himself because he has a preunderstanding (*Vorverständnis*). Preunderstanding refers to the life-relationship which the subject already has to the object of knowledge. To understand anything, argues Bultmann, man must pose a question about that which he hopes to understand. This raising of the question implies a kind of hidden understanding, since without some latent knowledge man cannot even formulate his question. A person, for example, is unable to ask about the meaning of friendship unless he already knows what it is to have and be a friend. "Without a pre-understanding," writes Bultmann, "no one can ever understand what is said anywhere in literature about love or friendship, or life and death—or, in short, about man generally." [4]

Now for Bultmann, this preunderstanding implies more than the mere presupposition for interrogating antique texts. Beneath all the various inquiries lies a basic question: What is the meaning of human existence? Since every man asks this question, though it may remain hidden in his heart, a sort of preunderstanding of his own existence is implied. In other words, man has a latent understanding of himself. This understanding, however, is inadequate, for it remains silent, muffled

by inauthenticity. The task of theology, indeed of biblical
exegesis, is to bring this muted self-understanding to clear
articulation. Since man has a preunderstanding of his
existence, however inadequate, he is able to appropriate
authentic self-understanding. This means that there is a continuity between the previous understanding and authentic
understanding of human existence. In short, man is a being
built for authentic existence.

The Doctrine of Man

Since understanding has to do with human existence, it is
apparent that the doctrine of man is basic to Bultmann's
theology. In presenting this doctrine, Bultmann is fond of
setting the biblical view against the backdrop of Hellenic
thought. The Greeks understand man as an element of nature.
For them, the cosmos is an ordered unity, and "man sees
himself as a particular instance of the general rule." [5] As a
facet of the natural order, man reflects the order of the
cosmos. He is a rational animal who can obey the laws of
nature. This rationality of man is basic to his being, for the
Greeks conceive "the nature of man as mind, as reason." [6]
Since man is essentially mind or spirit, death holds no ultimate terror for him. Death is a kind of graduation exercise
whereby man's essential spirit is promoted to a higher order.
For the Bible, on the other hand, man is not viewed in relation
to nature, but to God. Man is conceived as a creature formed
by the Creator, as an individual responsible to God. As a
responsible individual, man is not understood essentially as
mind, but as will. This kind of volitional creature grasps his
meaning in his decisions—decisions about his being which
determine his destiny. Consequently, Bultmann can interpret
Jesus' proclamation of the kingdom as a call to obedience
which makes possible authentic existence.

However, if the nature of man is discovered in his decision before God, it is clear that Bultmann's anthropology can only be illuminated in the light of his vision of God. As a matter of fact, Bultmann claims that "every assertion about God is simultaneously an assertion about man and vice versa." [7] What does Bultmann say about God that clarifies his understanding of man? Offhand, the answer may seem to be "Not much!" for Bultmann refers to "the impossible task of *speaking of God*." [8] The task is impossible because God is not an object which can be spoken about. Speaking about God implies that God is a thing like a clod or a crystal which can be weighed and measured. Only in response to revelation, only in the experience of God's presence, is it possible for man to speak of God. Speaking of God, therefore, is confessional. While acknowledging the possible existence of "many gods and many lords," Paul confesses, "*for us* there is one God, the Father, from whom are all things and for whom we exist" (1 Cor. 8:6, italics mine). Thus, man can speak of God only in terms of his own existence. "Therefore," says Bultmann, "the truth holds that when the question is raised of how any speaking of God can be possible, the answer must be, it is only possible as talk of ourselves." [9]

The fact that man can only speak of God in anthropological language does not mean that Bultmann has sold his theistic birthright for a mess of humanistic or pantheistic pottage. It does not mean that God is to be reduced to human subjectivity or that God's existence is relegated to action in the world which man may perceive as divine. As Bultmann says, "The fact that God cannot be seen or apprehended apart from faith does not mean that He does not exist apart from faith." [10] The necessity of confessional-existential speaking about God, in other words, does not exhaust God's transcendence. One interpreter discovers the underlying dialectic of Bultmann's thought to be expressed in Kierkegaard's famous idea of the infinite qualitative distinction between time and eternity,[11] that is, in the conviction that the world and God are separated by a chasm which man's effort cannot bridge. The implicit transcendence is often expressed in Bultmann's concept of God as the God of the future. This means that God is not ensnared in the past nor ready at hand to run man's errands like some cosmic bellhop; it means that God is ever before and beyond us—the God whose ways are not our ways.

When one speaks confessionally about the transcendent God, what can he say? How is it possible to speak in the present about the God of the future? Some critics have argued that such talk must be in signs and symbols and therefore is of necessity "mythological." Bultmann, while maintaining that objective speaking about God is impossible, argues that valid speech about God is not in his sense mythological, but analogical. The analogy most appropriate to describe God's being is the analogy of God as Father. From this analogy all mythological trappings such as the physical relation of the child to the father have been stripped away, so that the analogy remains a powerful expression of the reality of the divine-human relationship at the deepest personal level. Such an analogy does not simply symbolize man's relation to God; it actually expresses the presence of God in terms most meaningful for human existence—in terms of care and concern, love and forgiveness. Bultmann, therefore, does not abandon all theistic language; he understands it existentially.

What do these Bultmannian assertions about God say about the nature of man? For one thing, it is clear that man, like God, cannot be understood as an object. One does not come to know a person by memorizing his vital statistics, but rather through personal encounter, by taking the risk of having and being a friend. The true being of man, like the transcendence of God, is not some objective possession—an eternal spirit, some cosmic spark of the divine fire. Rather, man's existence is discerned in the possibility of authentic existence—a possibility which comes to him out of a future which is implicit in every decision. In other words, man must be understood in terms of the existentialist analysis of existence. This analysis for Bultmann, however, is conceived in theological terms, for the question of authenticity and the question of God are one and the same question.

Because of this theological understanding, Bultmann is able to present his anthropology under two headings: First, man prior to the revelation of faith, and second, man under faith. The second topic presupposes Bultmann's idea of revelation and will be explicated in the next chapter. The first—man before faith—is an exposition of Heideggerian anthropology in the language of Paul. Bultmann begins his analysis of Paul's anthropological terms with a discussion of the word *soma*, usually translated "body." According to Bultmann, *soma* is the most comprehensive word which Paul uses to describe human existence. "Man does not *have a soma*; he *is soma*." [12] Thus, the word *soma* is the equivalent of "self" or "person," and the self which *soma* describes can be either the subject or the object of man's action. This means that man can make decisions about himself: man is responsible. In existentialist terms, man is a being who can choose authentic or inauthentic existence.

For all the exegetical embellishments, Bultmann's analysis of Pauline anthropological terms is cut to the pattern of existentialist ontology. The situation of man before faith, however, is still more problematic. While existentialist philosophy can present an adequate ontological analysis of

man's existence, it cannot provide a remedy for man's ontic
condition. That is, existentialist philosophy can provide a
general understanding of the nature of man, but it cannot
afford an adequate solution to the problem of particular man
in his concrete situation. Whereas Heidegger believes man's
mere acceptance of his condition releases him for authentic
existence, Bultmann insists that man's predicament has
imposed a paralysis upon him; the way of escape can only
be opened from the outside. Bultmann presents this seriousness of man's ontic condition under the Pauline themes
"flesh," "sin," and "the world." Played together, these
themes sound a symphony in a minor key, for *"Man has
always missed the existence that at heart he seeks,* his intent
is basically perverse, evil." [13]

The term *flesh* (*sarx*) describes the earthly in contrast to
the divine. To live "according to the flesh" means to take
the earthly as norm—to live "in the pursuit of the merely
human, the earthly-transitory." [14] Life according to the flesh
is not simply mistaken, it is sinful. In Bultmann's judgment,
sin is man's extreme self-reliance, his effort to master his own
destiny and to create security by his own effort. Sin achieves
its supreme expression in man's boasting—a sort of egocentric chest-beating which isn't even interrupted by a cough.
The seriousness of man's situation is seen in Paul's personi-
fication of "flesh" and "sin" as *"powers to which man has
fallen victim* and against which he is powerless." [15] Man's
frantic struggle to gain release has only tightened the bonds
of slavery to sin. The struggle is ultimately futile, for *"sin
leads with inner necessity into death."* [16] The universality of
death supports the Pauline conviction that sin is universal.
Although Romans 5:12–19 seems to suggest that humanity's
sin is the consequence of the sin of Adam, Paul never

abandons the conviction that man is responsible—a concept presupposed by his whole argument in Romans 1–3 concerning the failure of Gentile and Jewish righteousness. The universality of sin is not the product of biological inheritance, but rather is the by-product of man's situation in the world. Man is born into a world dominated by evil forces where striving for self-security is inevitable; he "has let the threatening and tempting world become lord over him." [17]

The importance of existentialism for Bultmann's anthropology is now apparent. In both existentialist philosophy and Bultmannian theology the focus is upon man. Bultmann borrows existentialist method and terminology for his analysis of human existence. On the basis of this analysis, he agrees that man is a being of possibility—the possibility of authentic or inauthentic existence. This possibility is constantly confronting man with decisions about the future. Like Heidegger, Bultmann is pessimistic about man's response. Man inevitably makes the wrong decision. Bultmann, however, construes the consequence of this mistake as more serious than Heidegger. For the latter, man can overcome inauthentic existence by his own decision—by heroically embracing the fact that he is a being hurtling toward death. For Bultmann, only the existentialist diagnosis is correct; the prescription cannot effect the cure. Man is caught in sin, enslaved to the world, destined for a death which is the last enemy of man's existence. Man cannot flee inauthenticity by his own effort. "In short," says Bultmann, "he is a totally fallen being." [18]

The Idea of History

Closely allied with his doctrine of man is Bultmann's understanding of history. Again, he finds the contrast between

Greek and biblical views instructive. The former understands
history as a part of nature. The events of history, like natural happenings, are mere fragments of a cosmic pattern—
incidental variations of an unchanging design. Since there is
a natural order in history, moral and political lessons can be
learned from the past. For the Old Testament, on the other
hand, history is the arena where God is at work. Because God
works through his people to accomplish his purposes, the
study of history is of ultimate significance for man. "Therefore historiography is not a means of education for politi-
cians," writes Bultmann, "but a sermon to the people." [19]
Through the study of the past the promises of God can be
confirmed. The fulfillment of these promises, however, is con-
tingent on human responsibility. Thus, the announcement of
the promise is not a siren song to security, but a herald's call
to obedience.

This call of history, this herald of human responsibility,
indicates that for the Bible and for Bultmann the center of
history is man. History is not concerned with natural events
or world epochs but with the individual. "The decisive history is not the history of the world, of the people of Israel
and of the other people, but the history which everyone expe-
riences himself." [20] Thus the aim of the study of history is
self-understanding. This self-understanding, as we have seen,
is seized by man's decision in facing the future. Man never
arrives; he is always on the way. His authentic existence can
be lost or gained by his present decisions about the future.
Consequently, history acquires its importance as the stage
where man plays his decisive role.

Basic to Bultmann's understanding of history is the distinction between the German words *Historie* and *Geschichte*.
The former has to do with the sheer events of history—the

raw material which the historian uses in constructing the chronology of the past. *Geschichte,* on the other hand, has to do with the significance of events for man—the truth that history can declare the call to decision, provide the possibility of authentic existence. The difference between these two perspectives on history is illustrated by Bultmann's interpretation of the crucifixion of Jesus. That the cross is a factual event within *Historie* can be taken for granted. However, for the cross to take on historical significance—for the cross to be grasped as *geschichtlich* event— it must confront man with a decision about himself, with a decision as to whether he will let his future be determined by the power of the cross. "To believe in the cross of Christ does not mean to concern ourselves . . . with an objective event turned by God to our advantage, but rather to make the cross of Christ our own, to undergo crucifixion with him." [21]

Nevertheless, the *geschichtlich* event does not lose its character as event, since it is understood as essentially an act of God. In less theological and more philosophical language, the *geschichtlich* event is existential event. Moreover, the *geschichtlich* event has its original locus within the *historisch* event, and that is why, in spite of the misunderstanding of some of his critics, Bultmann continues to take the fact of the historical Jesus seriously. *Geschichtlich* event cannot be separated from *historisch* event, for *geschichtlich* event occurs in and through the *historisch*. This relationship is significant for Bultmann's understanding of God's action in history. As his novel interpretation of miracles shows, a *Wunder* (wonder) is not a unique event attributed to supernatural causality (that would be a miracle), but an action of God within a historical event which is perceptible to the eyes of faith. In other words, a *historisch* happening becomes a *geschichtlich*

event when the man of faith perceives in it an action of God—
an action which has ultimate significance for his own existence.

Since man finds his true existence in facing the future, it
is clear that the future is an important facet of Bultmann's
reflection on history. In biblical terms, this means that eschatology is crucial to historical understanding. The roots of
eschatological thinking found fertile soil in the Old Testament. There God's action in history was viewed as moving
toward a goal: God's promises would be fulfilled at the end
of history. Man was called to obey the conditions of the
promises in order to experience the joy of the end time. In
later Judaism, however, the prophetic idea of the God of the
future demanding responsibility in the present was swallowed
up in apocalyptic. The challenge of the future was betrayed
by the notion of a future fixed by a cosmic timetable. All
history was split into two epochs—the present evil age and
the glorious future. The future was separated from the present by a barrier which man's decision could not cross. Only
a cataclysmic act of God, only supernatural intervention,
could usher in the new age. The future had lost its meaning
for the present, and man could only twiddle his apocalyptic
fingers and await the catastrophic intervention of God.

This apocalyptic picture with its gaudy symbolism was
highly popular in the time of Christian origins. Jesus' claim
that he had seen "Satan fall like lightning" (Luke 10:18)
indicates that he was steeped in this sort of speculation. Paul,
too, cut his theological teeth on this kind of eschatological
fare. His description of the end is replete with trumpet calls
and angel shouts, judgment seats, clouds, and other apocalyptic paraphernalia. Both Jesus and Paul, however, qualified
their apocalyptic teachings. Jesus stressed the imminence of

the eschatological events, declaring that the reign of God was at hand. More important, he believed this nearness of the end demanded a decision of man in the present. Now is the time when man who sets his hand to the plow dare not look back, when the dead must be left to bury the dead. In Bultmann's words, "The Kingdom of God is a power *which, although it is entirely future, wholly determines the present.*" [22] Similarly, Paul, while continuing to depict the future in apocalyptic colors, believed the crucial eschatological event had occurred in the immediate past. "To be sure," writes Bultmann, "Paul still expected the end of the world as a cosmic drama . . . but with the resurrection of Christ the decisive event had already happened." [23] Besides, this event of the past confronts man with a present decision about the future. In the word of preaching, the eschatological Christ-event is the present encountering man. The day of salvation is not to take place in some distant future, but in the *now* of the proclamation of the word of reconciliation (2 Cor. 6:2).

Bultmann's way of interpreting biblical eschatology indicates that the present is the primary concern of his idea of history. Evidence for this is seen in Bultmann's effort to reduce the futuristic features of the New Testament picture of the end. Paul's notion of the final judgment, for example, is regarded as an unfortunate apocalyptic hangover. More sober is the eschatological thought of John, whose Gospel, when viewed in its original form, excludes futuristic elements completely. For the writer of the Fourth Gospel, judgment is confined to the present encounter with the Christ of faith, for "this is the judgment, that the light has come into the world, and men loved darkness rather than light" (John 3:19). The New Testament, according to Bultmann, stresses neither past nor future, but the time in between. "Therefore, the time be-

tween the resurrection of Christ and his expected Parousia,
has not only chronological but also essential meaning." [24] The
chronological meaning, however, is inconsequential, and Bultmann's central concern is the essential, or we may say, the
existential meaning. For faith, history in the chronological
sense has come to an end, for "Christ being the end of the
Law is at the same time the end of history." [25] The present,
therefore, is not a particular time in history, but a time in
man's existence—a time when the event of salvation which
transcends history can be actualized. The salvation event,
says Bultmann, "stands as it were outside of time and is valid
for every future in an eternal present." [26]

Bultmann's understanding of history, therefore, is essentially existentialist. This is why eschatology plays a leading
role in Bultmann's thought. Biblical eschatology, when subjected to Bultmann's exegesis, makes possible an existentialist
interpretation of history and man. This interpretation of man
and history, when presented in terms of eschatology, makes
possible the belief that existentialist theology is biblical. Indeed, for Bultmann, the existential event and the eschatological event are one and the same—an event of the present
wherein man is confronted with a decision about his existence.
Viewed from this existentialist perspective, the future has its
meaning in relation to the present decision; it presents man
with the possibility of authentic self-understanding. In so
doing, it is always open and never fixed by some apocalyptic
calendar. The present, the focal point of existentialist preoccupation, can be given no date in time; it is the eschatological-
existential moment of decision, the moment of encounter with
the Christ of faith.

Since the eschatological-existential event occurs in history,
the problem of the interpretation of historical documents—

the so-called hermeneutical question—is of importance. Bultmann, while making use of tools sharpened by nineteenth-century historiography, is primarily concerned with the existential question: What is the meaning of the historical document for man's existence? Actually, the question of the meaning of human existence is basic to the message of the entire Bible. The interpreter is able to put this question to the New Testament because, as we have seen, man has a prior understanding of himself. Since that preunderstanding is always inadequate, the investigation of the text can correct the old, distorted self-understanding. The revised understanding, in turn, becomes the basis for putting the question anew. This process of beginning with a prior understanding which is modified in the encounter with the text so as to create a new self-understanding Bultmann calls the "hermeneutic circle." As the interpreter walks around this circle, "the interpretation of the text always goes hand in hand with the exegete's interpretation of himself," [27] always moving closer to the goal of authentic self-understanding. Obviously, this chummy hand-holding between interpreter and interpretation is a long stride away from nineteenth-century historical objectivity. "Only the historian who is excited by his participation in history," says Bultmann, "will be able to understand history." [28] It is evident that this sort of hermeneutic owes much to the philosophy of existentialism.

Existentialism and Twentieth-Century Theology

Just as existentialism excited the imagination of Rudolf Bultmann, so it cast its spell over the minds of other twentieth-century theologians. The Jewish philosopher Martin Buber, for instance, believes the objective way of viewing reality to be distorted. Instead of the subject-object approach to being, the "I-it" relationship, Buber proposes the "I-Thou" relationship—the understanding of reality from the perspective of the mutuality of personal communication.

The Roman Catholic lay theologian Gabriel Marcel, while disavowing identification as an existentialist, argues that the old way of recognizing God as the Primal Cause is wrongheaded. Instead of a search for a metaphysical ground of being, Marcel recommends the recovery of the mystery of existence. This recovery is possible because man has a sense of uneasiness or *inquiétude* (like Heidegger's anxiety) which affords a sensitivity to the grace of God.

The unorthodox Eastern Orthodox theologian Nicholas Berdyaev insists that truth is subjective and that God is existential reality. Man, the main image in Berdyaev's thought, has forfeited his authentic freedom by falling into the world of objectification. In spite of this fall, man maintains a freedom of will whereby he may flee the false world through response to the creativity of God which continues to operate in man's existence. Just as this view is reminiscent of Bultmann's vision of the world, so H. Richard Niebuhr's contrast between outer and inner history provides a parallel to the Bultmannian distinction between *Historie* and *Geschichte*.

Perhaps the existentialist theologian who has most affected American thought is Paul Tillich. Influenced by Kierkegaard and Heidegger, Tillich displays certain similarities to Bultmann. He draws a sharp line between philosophy and theology, insisting that the former is concerned with ontology, the structure of being, while the latter explicates the meaning of existence for man. This approach, which employs philosophy to define the question and theology to provide the answer, is called the "method of correlation." It resembles Bultmann's desire to embrace existentialist analysis while remaining faithful to theological conclusions. Like Bultmann, Tillich is preoccupied with the being of man, and like Heidegger, he emphasizes the finitude of man. Faced with his finitude—the threat of nonbeing or nothingness—man lives under the shadow of anxiety. Nevertheless, in a manner reminiscent of Heidegger, Tillich asserts that man has the courage to affirm his finitude—"the courage to take the anxiety of meaninglessness upon oneself." [29]

Like Heidegger and Bultmann, Tillich is concerned with the meaning of history. History is always moving toward a goal, and in history man encounters God's purposes and call to decision. This idea of history involving a decision is clarified by Tillich's idea of *kairos*, a Greek word for "time," which Tillich uses to depict a decisive time, the moment when the eternal breaks into history. The *kairos*, like Bultmann's eschatological event, demands decision. In this moment of decision, man catches a glimpse of the kingdom of God and this vision illuminates his being. The kingdom can never be actualized in history, for it transcends the historical and points to God's purposes beyond history.

When one turns to biblical theology, unqualified representatives of an existentialist approach are more difficult to identify. Of course, the disciples of Bultmann, scholars like Günther Bornkamm and Hans Conzelmann, continued to pursue exegetical work on the basis of Heideggerian presuppositions. In this country, impetus was given to existential interpretation by the sojourn of Erich Dinkler at Yale in the early 1950s. Why this sort of theology evoked an enthusiastic response in America has often been asked. Did not existentialism ignite and flash like lightning across the dark skies of the Europe of the World War era—a Europe overshadowed by the clouds of political and moral crisis? Surely the American version would be a pale reflection—a small spark, mirrored in a glass darkly. This response, while containing an element of truth, fails to recognize that America, too, was facing crises. Moreover, the very empiricism and pragmatism which on the one hand seemed to blunt the edge of a theology forged in crisis served at the same time to blaze the trail of existentialism's success. It seemed to represent a theology girded for action rather than speculation—a theology of responsible deeds rather than abstract theories. Besides, the American tradition of revivalism with its strong emotional appeal and its fervent call to decision heard a responsive note in existentialism's concern for man's predicament and its demand for an either/or. The belief that this call came to the concrete individual in his particular situation seemed only another verse of the saga of individualism sung on the American frontier.

Actually, existentialism ventured beyond the walls of academe into the public forum; it became a popular philosophy. Many people who had never studied philosophy were captivated by the plays of Sartre and the novels of André Gide. The works of Dostoevsky and the short stories of Franz Kafka enjoyed a revival. George Buttrick, a popular preacher, went about the country lecturing on Camus's *The Fall*, while a sermon of Paul Scherer declared:

> It is not in an I-it relationship that we stand any more, the *I* over here and the *It* of God's good news over there. The relationship now is between an I and the Thou of God's good news in Christ—which incidentally would seem to provide sufficient justification for holding, without being obscurantist, that metaphysics, whatever else it is, is not the way to the holy.[30]

Many ministers considerably less sophisticated than Buttrick and Scherer were entranced by existentialism's supposed simplicity. Existentialism seemed to avoid the complications of metaphysics and the technicalities of logic. A philosophy wherein truth was discerned in one's own decision seemed to shrink the specter of theology. It was rather like the little boy playing checkers whose first moves were designed simply to trade men, but once the board was down to size, he really began to play! Obviously, amateurs who attempted a parallel theological method had never read Heidegger, let alone understood him. They supposed that existentialism provided a do-it-yourself theology which did not need to give a reason for the hope that was within.

In contrast to this simplistic view is the work of Amos Wilder, which reflects the influence of existentialism on American biblical theology. Educated in the Chicago school of sociohistorical criticism, Wilder is critical of a rationalistic historicism which presents Christianity as "doctrinaire and unrelated to life." [31] It is this sensitivity to life which draws Wilder into the existentialist orbit. Like Bultmann, he is concerned with man in his historical context. Ultimately, man has his meaning in relation to God. "It is the heart, will, obedience, action, which define the man and condition the work of God in him and through him." [32] Like Bultmann, Wilder is fascinated by the problem of history and eschatology. In interpreting the biblical doctrine of the end, Wilder is anxious to eschew all other-worldliness. The eschatological images of the New Testament are viewed as colorful symbols which speak vitally to man in his historical setting. Jesus' idea of the kingdom, for instance, "did not mean the 'end of the world' or the dissolution of the creation, but rather the transformation of the creation." [33] Consequently, "apocalyptic symbols could be used to represent what we call earthly events." [34] In advocating this anthropological perspective on eschatology, Wilder is able to see eye-to-eye with his colleague from Marburg: "The great value of Bultmann's view is that he refuses to allow the Cross and the Resurrection to be for us an external spectacle. We must identify ourselves with them in faith, by dying and rising with Christ ourselves." [35]

While Wilder was professing this existentialist posture at Chicago and Harvard, Paul Minear was assuming a similar stance at Andover-Newton and Yale. Like Bultmann, Minear addresses himself to the doctrine of man. Man has his meaning in relation to God, for "to be known by God is the precondition of authentic self-consciousness." [36] At the same time, monotheism finds its meaning in the decision of man, "when one God becomes the decisive reality for a particular man." [37]

It is in the realm of hermeneutics and eschatology, however, that parallels between Minear and Bultmann become apparent. Minear believes the understanding of the Bible requires a special historiography based on biblical eschatology. While this plea for a special methodology counters Bultmann's claim that the Bible needs no unique hermeneutic, Minear's reading of biblical eschatology is sufficiently existentialist to provide points of contact. History, in his view, can be understood only from the perspective of the decisive event within history, for "historical time is transformed by the actual appearance within time of an event which is ultimate." [38] The ultimate event is the event of God's action in Christ. This means that a Christocentric hermeneutic is required. The cross of Christ has put to death the old way of viewing history, and faith in Christ brings to life a new way of historical understanding. Like Bultmann, Minear interprets biblical eschatology in terms of man's decision of faith. The images of the Apocalypse, for example, depict neither eschatological happenings of the future, nor historical events of the present; they symbolize the prophet's struggle with the transcendent power of good and evil in his own existence. Thus for Minear, as for Bultmann, the crucial eschatological event occurs in the present existence of man. "The decisive turning point from death to life is determined," he says, "not by what happens in the grave, but by what happens now." [39]

Existentialism and the Christ of Faith

It is now apparent that existentialism is of vital importance for the theology of the midtwentieth century. Not only did this sort of thought invade the bastions of systematic and philosophical theology, it also triumphed as a popular philosophy, heralded by preachers and celebrated in the marketplace. In particular, biblical theologians who found it appropriate for considering central themes of the Bible were content to sojourn for a time in the house of being. When they moved in, they discovered that Rudolf Bultmann had already taken up residence. Bultmann, in other words, had anticipated the activity of many other theologians by appropriating a philosophical movement which was to become dominant in the intellectual life of the 1950s.

In adopting existentialism Bultmann was not doing something unique. His distinction is seen in his ability to employ a popular philosophy in his construction of a unique theological synthesis. Bultmann is thus able to speak with compelling relevance to the issues which occupy modern man. This is seen in the fact that for Bultmann the problem of man is *the* problem of theology; theology is anthropology. Yet, not only is man the central concern of contemporary thought, the question of the meaning of human existence is *the* question of the Bible. Thus the problem of man is the point at which existentialism and the word of the New Testament intersect— a point of correlation which reveals that the biblical message is crucial for modern man.

The question can be raised, of course, as to whether Bultmann's theology is simply existentialist philosophy in biblical clothing. In Bultmann's care, for example, the futuristic branch of New Testament eschatology has been pruned away. One of his students was once heard to remark that the second volume of his *Theology of the New Testament* is little more than existentialist theology with illustrations from the Fourth Gospel. Regardless of the validity of this charge, it is clear that Bultmann's intention is something different. He insists that "there will never be a right philosophy," [40] and argues that his adoption of existentialism represents only a methodological decision. Existentialism is adopted because it "offers the most adequate perspective and conceptions for understanding human existence." [41] Moreover, since the question of human existence is basic to the Bible, existentialism provides the hermeneutical key to biblical interpretation.

In spite of Bultmann's intention to employ existentialism as a mere method, the question can be asked: Does Bultmann's choice of existentialist tools determine the shape of his theological structure? This question is formulated by Schubert Ogden in terms of a distinction between existentialism's formal and material role in Bultmann's thought. "As Bultmann usually speaks of it," writes Ogden, "philosophy is understood to have strictly formal function, in the sense of being an ontological analysis of the phenomenon of existence as such. Yet . . . many of his statements presuppose that philosophy has a material significance as well." [42] In particular, Ogden argues that the distinction between authentic and inauthentic existence, drawn from existentialist philosophy, introduces material content into Bultmann's system, since it specifies how man must act in order for his existence to be authentic rather than inauthentic. Besides, Bultmann's preoccupation with man—his understanding of theology as anthropology—results from his adoption of the existentialist method. It is by means of this method that Bultmann has decided that the problem of human existence is the central question of the Bible. No one should know better than Bultmann that the way one puts the question determines the answer. To embrace existentialist method is to marry existentialist philosophy. This is confirmed by Bultmann's surprising conclusion that "the philosophers are saying the same thing as the New Testament and saying it quite independently." [43]

However, even Bultmann's critics recognize that his theology includes one basic element which is not borrowed from Heidegger: the conviction that the transition from inauthentic to authentic existence requires an act of God. This conviction involves Bultmann's view of the seriousness of sin and the tragedy of the human predicament. As a remedy for this situation Bultmann turns from the speculation of the philosophers to the gospel of the New Testament, for "the latter affirms the total incapacity of man to release himself from this fallen state." [44] This preference for the New Testament message underscores Bultmann's intention to be a biblical theologian, and explains his belief that the primary task of theology is the interpretation of the biblical message. Moreover, the biblical understanding of the redemptive action of God as occurring in history provides the ground for Bultmann's insistence on the necessity of the historicity of God's action in Jesus Christ—a concrete fact of history which cannot be swallowed up in timeless present.

Nevertheless, Bultmann, like Minear and Wilder, is not content to tarry long at the shrine of the historical Jesus. Though essential to the redemptive event, the Christ according to the flesh cannot be the ground for contemporary faith. God's redeeming action cannot be relegated to the distant past but must recur in the present of man's existence. The Christology of the New Testament is neither a collection of historical data nor a compendium of theological doctrine; for the New Testament "christology is simultaneously soteriology." [45] Existentialism provides the theologians of the mid-twentieth century with the means whereby God's redemptive act in the past becomes the saving event of the present— whereby the Jesus of history is confessed as the Christ of faith. This is possible because man is a being built for authentic existence—a responsible being who finds his authentic existence in decision about God's act. It is possible because God's action has occurred in history—in the historical Jesus, yet also in the moment of God's continual encounter with man. It is possible because God's action is eschatological-existential event—the event of God's ultimate action enacted in history and reenacted in the word of proclamation. The passion of Bultmann's theological program is to speak that word with clarity so that modern man can hear and obey, to witness to the Word made flesh in Jesus so that contemporary man can have faith in Christ.

Chapter 4

Christ the Word

The Proclamation of Dialectical Theology

PROTESTANT THEOLOGY in the first half of the twentieth century is marked by a return to the message of the Reformation. Confronted with the crises of the time, theologians were seeking some sure ground in their religious heritage. As contemporary culture crumbled about them, they looked for a "city which has foundations, whose builder and maker is God" (Heb. 11:10). The foundations, to be sure, were not to be found in the religion of the time, for that faith was a structural element in the crumbling culture. The sort of theology then espoused by the universities, with its cold commitment to scientific method and deep devotion to human reason, had spawned an intellectual cult whose god was molded in the image of man.

Karl Barth, the Moses of the new Protestantism, found that much of what he had learned at Berlin and Marburg was not basic to the sure foundation. As he mounted the pulpit in the village church at Safenwil, Barth discerned that

the salvation of his Swiss parishioners did not depend on the
documentary hypothesis concerning the Pentateuch nor the
latest solution to the synoptic problem. Instead, his people
needed a word from God. This word, in Barth's conviction,
was to be heard in the Bible, and because of this conviction,
he began to study the Scriptures in a new way. The result was
a commentary on Romans, *Der Römerbrief*, published in
English as *The Epistle to the Romans*, probably the most significant theological work of the first half of the twentieth
century.

In contrast to the scientific commentaries of the day with
their concern for historical criticism, Barth's work was starkly
theological. To historical criticism he conceded a place, but
confessed that if forced to choose between it and the older
doctrine of inspiration, he would select the latter. Barth's
intention was to go beyond the historical to the "spirit of the
Bible." [1] The resulting "spiritual" hermeneutic provided the
clue to the discovery of the "strange new world" of the Bible.
In that world, the interpreter could hear the voice of Paul
afresh—a voice which spoke not only to the Christians of
first-century Rome, but also to the church of twentieth-century
Europe.

In opposition to a religion which had been accommodated
to culture, Barth proclaimed a theology of the Word of God.
This theology announced the transcendence of God instead of
his immanence, the sinfulness of man rather than his good-
ness. At base, these beliefs rested on Kierkegaard's idea of
the "infinite qualitative distinction" between time and eternity, as Barth was to acknowledge in the preface to the second
edition of his commentary. The resulting dialectic—that God
was in heaven and man on earth—became the ontological
ground of the new theology. Since man could not cross the

great chasm which the Creator had fixed between himself and his creation, knowledge of God could only come by means of God's initiative, by revelation. God made himself known in the declaration of his Word—a dynamic event which called man to judgment and repentance. In Jesus Christ this Word became flesh, and to this Christ the Scriptures bear witness. This stress on the Scriptures and the theology of the Word represented a return to the claims of the Reformation. Consequently, the new theology was sometimes called neo-Reformation theology or neoorthodoxy. Looking back on the early days of the new movement, Barth was later to reflect that he had been like a man ascending the tower of the church. Groping in the dark, he had reached for the railing to steady himself, but instead caught hold of the bell rope. The tolling of the bell became a call to action heard round the theological world.

Among the first to respond to the call was Barth's fellow countryman, Emil Brunner. In a favorable review of Barth's *Romans*, Brunner was critical of contemporary biblical studies which had "overlooked the essential." [2] That essential was not to be discovered by scientific study, but, as Barth declared, by listening for the Word of God announced in the Bible. In Jesus Christ that Word had come to man as a person, and to this personal revelation the only appropriate response was faith. Although theological differences were later to cause a rift between Brunner and Barth, they remained one in a common quest of the Christ of faith. In Barth's words, "I had to learn that Christian doctrine, if it is to merit its name and if it is to build up the Christian church in the world as she must needs be built up, has to be exclusively and conclusively the doctrine of Jesus Christ—of Jesus Christ as the living Word of God spoken to us men." [3]

Another affirmative vote was cast by Rudolf Bultmann. In his review of the second edition to Barth's *Romans*, Bultmann acknowledged that "basically I believe I am one with Barth." [4] According to Bultmann, Barth had raised the right question: What is the essence of faith? Barth had answered that authentic faith is not moved by religious feelings nor attained by mystical endeavor. Faith is granted by the act of God—the act which breaks into history to judge the world and confront man with a crisis. Only the man who stands naked before God, stripped of all pretense, is able to respond in faith. Such radical trust in God is no human work, but man's risk of himself—"a leap into the void." [5] In spite of later disagreements between the two theologians, Bultmann maintains that his entire theological effort has been exerted merely to clarify and secure the method presupposed by Barth's *Romans*. Since Barth's position has actually undergone a shift in the meantime, it may well be that Bultmann has remained since the 1920s the most consistent advocate of dialectical theology. The story has been told that when they met after World War II, Bultmann responded to all Barth's queries by repeating, "I stand where you stood." [6]

Elements of Dialectical Theology in the Thought of Rudolf Bultmann

Bultmann's migration from the level plain of liberalism to the steep crags of dialectical theology was more gradual than Barth's. The young Bultmann had been, along with his father, a member of the liberal theological group, the Friends of the Christian World, and some of his earliest essays appear in their journal, *Die Christliche Welt*. These early works quote Schleiermacher with approval and display a loyalty to liberalism's historical-critical approach. This loyalty, while becoming a point of contention between himself and Barth, continued to play a major role in Bultmann's remaining career. Many years later he was to confess that "I have endeavored throughout my entire work to carry further the tradition of historical-critical research as it was practiced by the 'liberal' theology." [7] Yet, while the historical critical method could sever the bonds of orthodoxy to free man in the quest for truth, in Bultmann's hands its sharp edge could cut to the root of liberalism's easy presuppositions. It could show, for example, that the faith of liberalism, supposedly based on factual certainty, rested instead on historical relativity. Bultmann's sensitivity to liberalism's relativity led to his estrangement from the Friends of the Christian World and his association with the dialectical theologians.

It is clear that the fundamental dialectic—the infinite qualitative distinction between time and eternity—is the common ground on which the early Barth and the inveterate Bultmann stand. From this dialectic stem Bultmann's ideas of the God who cannot be confused with the world and of man whose existence has meaning only in relation to God, the view of revelation as nonobjective, faith as risk, exegesis as independent of every world view. The fact that the dialectic is borrowed from Kierkegaard and the fact that Barth confessed he had been reading Dostoevsky make it evident that early dialectical theology is closely allied with existentialism. The type of existentialism involved, however, is expressly theistic, for it is concerned with the question of the ultimate meaning of existence. This question—the question about God—can only be answered existentially. "Nonexistential" theology is essentially irrelevant, since it understands God metaphysically and salvation doctrinally. The result is a God who

is both too remote (beyond man's existence) and too near
(trapped in objectivity), and a salvation which is both impotent (produced by man's effort) and external (distilled
into doctrinal statement). Instead, the dialectic must be taken
with radical seriousness, confessing a God who is both transcendent and revealed, and declaring a salvation which is at
the same time powerful (as God's act) and present (in man's
existence). For Bultmann, Heidegger's ontology was to become the means for further clarification of this dialectic. For
Barth, existentialism was to be viewed increasingly as the
philosophical stricture which limited the absolute of God's
Word.

Holy God and Human Sinner

Bultmann's doctrine of God is one pillar of the basic
dialectic, a central column in his theological structure. The
idea of God has already been discussed in relation to the
influence of existentialism upon Bultmann (see chapter 3).
There it was observed that God cannot be understood apart
from his relation to man and that speech about God except in
terms of man's existence is impossible. It is, however, appropriate to stress God's transcendence in analyzing the elements of dialectical theology in Bultmann's thought. Bultmann can describe God in terms of the famous Barthian
phrase as "wholly other." In a sermon of 1917, before
Barth's commentary had appeared, Bultmann declared that
"we always see God as wholly other than we thought him to
be," and referred to him as "the mysterious and hidden" [8]
God. In contrasting Christianity with humanism, Bultmann
writes, "God is the absolutely transcendent One, the Eternal
One, and his eternity is qualitatively different from everything of this world." [9]

Bultmann's doctrine of man, the other side of the dialectic, has also been discussed in relation to existentialist influences (see chapter 3). There it was observed that man is a being of responsibility who has chosen inauthentic existence, and while existentialist philosophy can depict man's captivity, it cannot provide the way of escape. The biblical word for this predicament—a word which strikes a responsive chord in dialectical theology—is *sin*. Man is a sinner who lives in the flesh, trapped in the world, destined for death. Yet, while Bultmann can speak of man as "a totally fallen being," he does not appear to advocate a doctrine of "total depravity." As some Catholic commentators have noted, Bultmann detects a continuity between man before and after faith—a continuity provided by the basic ontological structure of man's being. This concept of continuity, however, is not designed to diminish the idea of the seriousness of sin so dear to the dialectical theologians. This is evident in Bultmann's stress upon *sin* rather than *sins*—upon sin as a power which dominates man's life instead of particular errors into which the wayward man might wander. Therefore, Bultmann can say that *"real sin does not consist in individual transgressions of the law at all, but in the basic attitude of man—his striving to establish his own righteousness,* and to glorify himself in the presence of God." [10]

The Necessity of Revelation

Since God is holy and man is sinner, knowledge of God cannot be acquired by human effort. Only as God takes the initiative, only as God comes to man, only by revelation, can God be known. For the dialectical theologians, this revelation has nothing to do with a knowledge of God through the created order. Bultmann, for example, concludes that "there

is then no sense in speaking of the revelation of God in
nature." [11] This conclusion, for anyone who has been listening
to the potent preaching of the dialectical theologians, is self-
evident. How could God be discovered in nature when he is
by definition "wholly other"? Just as man cannot detect a
portrait of God in nature, he cannot find ultimate meaning
by peering into the ambiguities of history. It is likewise
mistaken to suppose that every religion reflects some facet of
the divine truth. "Faith," according to Bultmann, "rejects
the idea that God is revealed everywhere in religions and in
religious people." [12]

These attempts to find God by human effort follow the blind
alley of a false understanding of the nature of revelation.
They suppose that God is an object which can be observed and
thus deny his transcendence; they imagine that knowledge of
God is an intellectual mastery of data, and thus they deny its
power. Yet, once revelation is understood not as a communication of ideas but as a mediation of life, then the concept of
natural revelation can be reinterpreted. What man discovers
in nature is that the quest for the Omnipotent is futile and
man himself is impotent. What man learns from history is
that ultimate meaning is elusive and man himself is caught
in temporality. What man discerns in other religions is that
the transcendent God is hidden and man makes gods in his
own image. In short, what has been thought to be natural
revelation of God is in fact the revelation of man—man in his
limitation, man in need of God's revelation. This fundamental
need for revelation is the silencing of all other voices, the
preparation to hear the Word of God.

Revelation as Event

Since other forms of revelation merely clear the way
through the wilderness for the advent of God, Bultmann can

speak of the "exclusiveness of the Christian revelation." [13] This authentic revelation must be understood as event, as act of God. In biblical terms—terms familiar to Luther and the dialectical theologians—it can be called the Word of God. This Word, of course, must not be confused with human words; it is not something which can be written down and memorized. In keeping with the basic dialectic, God's Word is not manageable, but the act of the transcendent God who breaks into history, shattering man's structures and conditions, encountering man in his innermost being. For the Old Testament, the Word is the powerful action which brings all things into existence, the mighty command that orders Israel out of Egypt.

"*In the New Testament,*" says Bultmann, "the only content of the Word of God is *Christ.*" [14] The Word of God spoken in the events of Israel's history has become flesh in Jesus Christ. This understanding of Christ as Word or event is designed to avoid the notion that man can manipulate God's revelation— that the divine action can become the object of historical investigation. Consequently, it is not possible to prove that Christ is the revelation of God, and the sheer historicity of Jesus serves to preclude any such proof. The scandal of Christianity is the indemonstrable conviction that the transcendent One has acted in this particular history. Such a claim is radical renunciation of any kind of empirical evidence or rational argument—a stumbling block to scientists and foolishness to philosophers.

As a matter of fact, the understanding of Jesus Christ as revelation of God is basic to the problem of the historical Jesus in the theology of Bultmann. On the one hand, the revealer is the definite person of history; on the other, he is the Word of the transcendent One. As that Word, Jesus can no longer be known as Christ according to the flesh (2 Cor.

5:16). Nevertheless, for the revelation of God to be revelation *to man*, Christ had to come in the flesh, into history. Consequently, Bultmann, in spite of charges of inconsistency and conservatism, has held tightly to the historical fact of revelation—what he calls the *Dass* or "that." Bultmann insists, however, that we cannot go beyond the fact *that* God acted to the "what" or "how" of revelation, because supplying such content would result in a flimsy human construction rather than the dynamic action of God. Actually, Bultmann's rigid grip on the *Dass* results from his understanding of the basic dialectic. If revelation is to be received it must come to man in history, therefore, as particular, concrete event. But if revelation is revelation *of God* it must be the action of the transcendent One. Thus, Jesus Christ is paradoxical or eschatological event—a historical event in which God acts.

This paradox is also articulated in answer to the question, What is the content of the revelatory event? Bultmann asserts that "the Word of God is *Christ*, his cross and resurrection." [15] Since *"faith in the resurrection is really the same thing* as faith in the saving efficacy of the cross," [16] it is evident that the historical content of the revelatory event is reduced basically to the crucifixion. Like Paul, Bultmann has decided to know nothing but Christ and him crucified (1 Cor. 2:2). He focuses attention on the crucifixion event because it magnifies the scandal—it exposes the incredibility of the historical revelation. Thus the scandal of the cross becomes a sign of the fundamental dialectic: a revelation which is both near (in man's history) and remote (beyond every form of historical expectation), both a revelation *to man* and a revelation *of God*. The problem of the historical Jesus in relation to the understanding of revelation is this: How can God reveal himself and still be God? Or in terms of the present discussion:

How can the basic dialectic be preserved? Bultmann answers: By a revelation which is itself dialectical, by a historical Jesus who is also Christ of faith.

Revelation as Word of Salvation

The dialectical shape of revelation is further clarified by Bultmann's view of Jesus Christ as "once-for-all" event. According to this view, God's revelatory act which occurred at one particular time in Jesus is effective for men in all times. This means that God's action in revelation, for all its historical particularity, cannot be restricted to antiquity. "For Paul," says Bultmann, "the cross of Christ is not simply an historical event belonging to a remote past, but an event which, initiated in Christ, penetrates the whole of human history." [17] But, how does the event which happened in the past become revelation for men removed from that historical happening? Bultmann replies that the once-for-all event is "continually re-enacted in the proclamation." [18] In other words, the proclamation or kerygma is itself God's revelatory action.

Yet, if the event of revelation which took place in the past continues to happen in history, has not revelation been transformed into a timeless truth? Does not the "for all" destroy the "once"? Implicit in these questions is the notion that a revelation which occurred once and continues to recur in history must involve a series of events which unveil some transhistorical, eternal truth about God. Bultmann reminds us, however, "that we are not speaking of an idea of God but of the living God . . . who encounters us here and now." [19] The important thing, as Bultmann's stress on the *Dass* makes clear, is *that* God acts, not *what* he does or *how* he acts. Moreover, God always acts in the concrete situation, so that each event

of revelation in terms of its "what" and "how" is in a sense
new. God's continuing action in history, just as his act in the
past, takes place in a particular "now." Thus, the revelation
of God in Christ reveals that revelation is always in the particular event, that neither in the past, nor in ongoing history is
revelation the disclosure of a timeless truth. Nevertheless,
there is a continuity in revelation—a continuity in the God
who acts, the same God who acted decisively in Jesus Christ.
"The paradox is that the word which is always happening
here and now is one and the same with the first word of the
apostolic preaching crystallized in the Scriptures of the New
Testament." [20]

What is the message which the apostles proclaimed?
According to Bultmann, it is: Jesus Christ. By this answer,
Bultmann does not mean that doctrine about Christ is
preached, but that Christ is proclaimed as saving event.
"Pauline Christology," like Bultmann's own, "is nothing
other than the proclamation of *the saving act of God which
took place in Christ*." [21] This is why Paul "does not specula-
tively discuss the metaphysical essence of Christ, or his relation to God, or his 'natures,' but speaks of him as the one
through whom God is working for the salvation of the world
and man." [22] Bultmann's doctrine of Christ, like his doctrine
of God, has its meaning in relation to man. The important
issue is not who Christ is, but what he does, or rather, what
God does through him. Consequently, Bultmann is fond of
quoting Melanchthon's famous dictum, "To know Christ is to
know the benefits he confers." In short, Christology is soteriology.

This identification of Christology and soteriology illuminates Bultmann's view of revelation. What is communicated
in revelation is not new ideas, but new life. To understand

how revelation gives life, it is necessary to investigate Bultmann's idea of salvation—an idea explicated under the Reformation rubric of justification by faith. For Bultmann, justification or righteousness is not an ethical but a forensic term. Man does not attain righteousness by moral effort; he is declared righteous by God. Since righteousness is something man receives from God and not something man does, it has its origin in God's grace. The grace of God, rather than being a divine attribute, is an act—the saving deed of God in Christ. What man could not do to free himself from sin God has done for him in the Christ event. For the man who is separated in time and space from the historical happening, the saving event recurs in the preaching and sacraments of the church. *"The salvation-occurrence,"* says Bultmann, *"is nowhere present except* in the proclaiming, accosting, demanding, and promising word of preaching." [23]

The word heard in apostolic preaching is echoed in the Bible. For Bultmann, the Scriptures, like the sacraments, are understood as kerygma. This means that the Bible is a dynamic proclamation, not a compendium of divine quotations. As Bultmann says, "The New Testament is the Word of God only indirectly and not directly." [24] As indirect Word, the revelation of God in the Bible cannot be construed as an objective body of data and doctrine whose truth can be demonstrated. "God's Word is hidden in the Scriptures as each action of God is hidden everywhere." [25] In other words, the basic dialectic is preserved: the Word of God is spoken in the Bible, but the words of the Bible cannot be identified as words of God. But how, then, is one to hear the Word of God in the Bible, to distinguish between the Word of God and the words of men? No rational criteria can be employed, of course, for that would involve the blasphemous claim that man can establish the Word of God. Only as the Word is received as event which encounters the hearer personally, as direct address, is the word of the Bible heard as Word of God. To be sure, only the man of faith can hear the word as personal address, but he knows most of all that the word is not dependent on his own decision, that the word is Word *of God*. More than this, the Bible has in itself a special quality as address. "What distinguishes the Bible from other literature," says Bultmann, "is that . . . the Bible becomes for me a word addressed personally to me, which not only informs me about existence in general, but gives me real existence." [26]

The Response of Faith

Integral to Bultmann's idea of revelation is his understanding of man's response. As we have seen, the concept of pre-understanding posits the conviction that man has the capacity to receive revelation, the ear to hear God's Word. This capacity, however, does not mean that receiving is a human accomplishment. Instead, it is sheer acceptance of God's accomplishment—what the Bible and the dialectical theologians call "faith." God's revelation, says Bultmann, "reveals life wherever it evokes the response of *faith*." [27] The priority of God's revelation is seen in the fact that faith itself can be understood as a gift. This stress on faith as acceptance of God's grace has led some Catholic critics to hear Bultmann's whole theological program as variations on the Lutheran theme of *sola fide*.

What is the nature of this faith which rejects human accomplishment? Bultmann answers in terms of Pauline theology. In essence, he says, faith is the "attitude of man in which he receives the gift of 'God's righteousness.'" The structure of faith includes five constitutive elements.

1. Faith is primarily *obedience*. Faith means silencing all other claims in order to hear the demand of God—"the obedient submission to the God-determined way of salvation."

2. Faith is at the same time *confession*. This means that faith has an object, that is, that faith is faith *in* something. The object, of course, is not some objective entity, for faith's object is God's saving activity in Christ.

3. Faith is also *hope*. Although a present reality, faith is always directed toward the future. "This 'hope,'" says Bultmann, "is the freedom for the future and the openness toward it which the man of faith has because he has turned over his anxiety about himself and his future to God in obedience."

4. The correlative of hope is fear; thus *fear* is an element in the structure of faith. Fear prevents the believer's fall into a false sense of security. In the balance between fear and hope, the man of faith walks the tightrope of a life stretched from a "no longer" to a "not yet." That is, he is no longer bound to the false securities of the past, but he has not yet reached the reality of the future fulfillment.

5. At the same time, faith means *confidence*. In the midst of the certain uncertainty, man continues to walk by faith, not by sight, in "complete surrender of one's own care and strength to God." [28]

Having analyzed the structure of faith, Bultmann proceeds to describe the life of faith. The man who has responded to God's revelation in faith has a new way of life. The life of faith, itself a gift of God's grace, is a life of new quality which can be characterized as the life "in Christ." This

suggests that the new life, which involves a genuine obedience
to God's demands, arises spontaneously out of the new
existence which God has given. Above all, the new life can be
characterized as a life in freedom. Through faith, man is
freed from sin so that he can walk in the Spirit. This means
that the power of the old life—the life in bondage to the
flesh and the world—is broken. From God, the believer has
received the gift of the Spirit, that is, the power of God at
work in man. Through this power man is enabled to obey the
will of God—a will which reaches its highest expression in
the command of love. Even this lofty command can be obeyed,
for the highest of all the spiritual gifts is granted to the
lowliest Christian—the gift of *agape* which manifests itself in
mundane deeds.

The life of freedom is free from all legalistic demands.
This does not mean that the life of faith is a life without ethical responsibility. On the contrary, only the man of faith
knows the depths of God's demand and only the man of freedom is able truly to be obedient. What he obeys is the law of
Christ—the law of love. This law manifests itself in every
encounter with the neighbor. When asked what the law
requires—what one must do to obey—Bultmann stolidly refuses to answer. To translate the law of Christ into some
ethical system would be to put the new wine of the spirit into
the old wineskins of legalism. The demand of love is absolute
and breaks every legalistic system. "If man really loves,"
says Bultmann, "he already knows what he has to do." [29]
To be sure, he will never obey the law of love completely,
for the life of faith is the life between the already and the
not yet. In this life, the Christian sees in part and obeys in
part and only hopes that the perfect will come.

Nevertheless, the life of faith is the eschatological life.

Already the believer participates in the new creation; already he tastes the fruit of the new age; already he has received the Spirit as downpayment on the new dwelling. Since he is free from sin, the man of faith is free from fear of its ultimate outcome, death. Although Bultmann consistently emphasizes the present realization of the eschatological expectation, and although he rigidly refuses to put concrete content into the hope for the future, he has not forsaken the Christian hope. The hope, however, is no pale projection of man's dream, but confidence in the purposes of God. "Therefore," says Bultmann, "this hope or this faith may be called readiness for the unknown future that God will give. In brief, it means to be open to God's future in the face of death and darkness." [30]

Dialectical Thought and Biblical Theology in Midtwentieth Century

The kind of theology Barth embraced in Basel and Bultmann espoused in Marburg became popular throughout the Protestant world. "A movement rather than a 'school,' " writes Langdon Gilkey, "neo-orthodoxy has influenced almost every contemporary theologian." [31] Indeed, the movement was so vigorous that observers of religious thought in midcentury could speak of a theological renaissance. In an era of crises—of wars and rumors of war—a theology which built crisis into its structure appeared ready to weather the storms of the time. The older liberalism, with its high hopes for man and bright confidence in social progress, had been dashed on the rocks of dictatorship and smothered in the gas chambers at Auschwitz. Once the shooting had ceased, the Confessing church which had resisted the Nazis exercised considerable influence in Germany. Theologians of that church, many of

them students of Barth and Bultmann, were granted promi-
nent teaching positions in the European universities. The more
America had been swept into a maelstrom across the sea, the
more it sought refuge in Continental theology.

Momentum was given to the new theological movement
when America produced a Barth of its own, Reinhold
Niebuhr. From his post at Union Seminary in New York,
Niebuhr became the most influential voice in American
theology during the decade of the 40s. Along with his brother
H. Richard of Yale, Niebuhr put his mark on a whole gen-
eration of divinity students. For our purposes, the striking
feature of Niebuhr's work is his commitment to what he calls
"the biblical view." While one of his critics charges that
Niebuhr "seems to wish to secure in this fashion . . . the
prestige and emotional appeal that to Christian readers are
associated with the Bible," [32] the truth of the matter is that
Niebuhr is reflecting the signs of his theological time. Dialectical theology gave birth to a theological era wherein the
importance of the Bible was taken for granted.

Like Bultmann, Niebuhr is deeply in debt to the biblical
understanding of man and history. Man, though made in the
image of God, is limited by his mortality. His attempt to
overcome this limitation by his own effort leads to sin. Sin,
according to Niebuhr, takes two forms: the sin of pride and
the sin of sensuality. The former includes intellectual, moral,
and spiritual pride, or what Bultmann, in Pauline terms,
would call boasting. The latter involves the effort to escape
self-love by a lust for other things, or what Bultmann, in
biblical terms, would call enslavement to the world. In
accordance with the reformers, Niebuhr rejects salvation by
works. Since sin is essentially pride and self-seeking, every
attempt to save oneself is essentially an egocentric and

therefore essentially sinful effort. Since egocentric endeavor is inevitable, Niebuhr agrees with dialectical theology that sin is universal. Like the dialectical theologians, Niebuhr is concerned with the meaning of history and is convinced that the biblical view is valid. From the vantage point of the Bible, God is seen as sovereign over history—a conviction which can only be established through revelation in particular events within history. For the Christian, the decisive revelatory event has occurred in Christ. The "final clue to the mystery of the divine power is found in the suffering love of a man on the Cross" [33]—a clue perceptible only to the eyes of faith. Equipped with this clue, Niebuhr joins in the quest of the Christ of faith.

The popularity of this kind of theology gave impetus to the study of the Bible. Consequently, the work of biblical scholars, many of whom were theological liberals with little sympathy for the new movement, was given encouragement. Men like H. J. Cadbury (Harvard), Millar Burrows (Yale), and F. C. Grant (Union) were blessed with a multitude of students. Yet, while the students were studying historical criticism with these masters, they were learning their theology from other voices in other rooms—from the Niebuhrs, from Barth and Brunner, from Rudolf Bultmann. At the same time, some biblical scholars were resonating to the new theological sounds. New Testament theologians like Otto Piper of Princeton and Floyd Filson of McCormick constituted what Brevard Childs has called "a distinctive Biblical Theology Movement." [34] Along with others, especially Old Testament scholars like Ernest Wright and Bernhard Anderson, these biblical theologians arrived at a consensus which includes, among other things, (1) rediscovery of the theological dimension of the Bible and reaffirmation of the relevance of biblical theology for modern man; (2) emphasis on the unity of the whole Bible, Old and New Testaments, without overlooking the diversity within this unity; (3) detection of the major theme of the Bible in God's action in history—a sequence of events constituting a *Heilsgeschichte*, the history of salvation.

Typical of the new movement was Bernhard Anderson's *Rediscovering the Bible*. The new discovery was made by sailing a straight course between the Scylla of fundamentalism and the Charybdis of liberalism. Since the new movement was being accused of biblicism and supernaturalism, the biblical theologians felt obliged to pledge their loyalty to the historical critical method. On the other hand, they were eager to disavow allegiance to liberalism's conclusions and to assert instead the belief that the Bible was an authoritative theological book. "It wouldn't be enough to say that the Bible is the record of *man's search for God,*" wrote Robert McAfee Brown. "It is much closer to the truth to say that *the Bible is the record of God's search for man.*" [35] According to Anderson, the Bible is bound together by a golden thread which runs from Genesis to Revelation—the story of the ongoing action of God in history for the salvation of mankind. The main act in God's redemptive pageant is Jesus Christ. "Early Christians," says Anderson, "took their stand on the faith that God had revealed the meaning of man's life at one point in human history: the life, death and resurrection of Jesus Christ—viewed as a single event—and the biblical drama which led up to that climactic, eternal moment." [36]

While Anderson's book was written for the popular audience, the American biblical theology movement is further illustrated by the work of G. Ernest Wright and Floyd V. Filson. These scholars believe that biblical theology has a primary role to play in the theological arena. The kind of theology which the Scriptures prescribe, however, is distinctively different from dogmatics. According to Wright, one of the errors of the past is that "Biblical theology has long been dominated by the interests of dogmatic or systematic theology." [37] Or, as Filson says, "The unique thing about the biblical message is found not in its system of ideas, but rather in the ongoing working of God in history." [38] In other words, biblical theology is history-of-salvation theology. This theology can be characterized by Wright as "confessional recital," for it consists in biblical man confessing faith by reciting what God has done in history for man's redemption. The supreme event in this history of salvation is Jesus Christ; he is the touchstone by which all else must be interpreted.

Actually the salvation-history theology represented by Wright and Filson had precursors on the Continent, particularly Ethelbert Stauffer and Oscar Cullmann. Stauffer's *New Testament Theology* appeared in 1941 and is written under the theme "the Christocentric theology of history in the New Testament." Presented in topical arrangement, it is virtually a systematic theology of the Bible—which also describes Alan Richardson's *An Introduction to the Theology of the New Testament* (1958). Cullmann's *Christ and Time* was first published in 1946 and defended at length in his more recent *Salvation in History*. Both Stauffer and Cullmann abandon natural theology in favor of a theology of divine disclosure. "Since no one can of himself come to God," writes Stauffer, revelation "can only happen by God's coming to us." [39] God comes to us in a series of historical events which find their fulfillment in Jesus Christ. This special revelation discloses the meaning of all history and witnesses to the absolute sovereignty of God.

For Cullmann, the history of salvation is to be explained in terms of the biblical understanding of time. In contrast to the philosophically colored concepts of time and eternity, the Bible views time as a sequence of events; that is, it maintains a linear view of time. This line of temporal happenings which stretches back before creation and reaches forward beyond the end of history finds its meaning at the midpoint: God's revelation in Jesus Christ. The time before the midpoint is the time of preparation, while the time after the midpoint is the time of fulfillment. Although it occurs a long time prior to the final fulfillment, the event at the midpoint does not lose its force as eschatological happening. Rather, it is like a decisive battle before the end of a war which shows in advance how sure the ultimate victory really is. The similarity of this scheme of divinely appointed events to the pattern of Jewish apocalyptic speculation is confirmed by Stauffer's claim that "the world of apocalyptic ideas is the one in which the NT writers were really at home." [40]

By now it is clear that salvation-history theology is not dialectical theology. According to the latter what is lacking in the former is a recognition of the basic dialectic. Rather than viewing the chasm between God and the world, the theologians of *Heilsgeschichte* have built a solid bridge between heaven and earth. Instead of the God who remains hidden in his revelation, whose action in history is perceptible only to faith, they present a God whose deeds can be identified with particular historical events open to the investigation of the historian. Instead of the God whose ways are not our ways, whose future is open to his own purposes, they depict the God whose ways are ascertained, whose future is captive to a predetermined plan.

If dialectical theology is so critical of salvation-history

theology, how are the two positively related? Basically, the answer is found in superficial similarities in their ideas of revelation. The salvation-history theologians agree that man in his sin and limitation cannot discover the high and holy God—that God can only be known as he makes himself known. God's revelation occurs in history, and the Bible is the primary witness to that historical revelation. What the salvation-history theologians have done against their own intention, however, is to transform this idea of revelation into a systematic theology of biblical history.

Nevertheless, the conviction that the supreme act of revelation has occurred in Jesus Christ offers a parallel to dialectical theology's confession of Christ as once-for-all event. The designation of Christ as the midpoint assumes a modern perspective. Whereas Paul viewed Christ as the end of history, the salvation-history theologians posit the midpoint on the basis of a long lapse of time since the original historical occurrence. This means that the modern perspective has contributed to the construction of the whole structure of salvation-history theology. Even though the acts of God are identified with particular objective events, the total pattern and meaning of *Heilsgeschichte* is sketched by the faith of the theologian. The recognition of Jesus Christ as the central figure and key to the understanding of the whole of history demands faith in Christ. While the implicit Christ of faith is one with the historical Jesus, it seems evident that sheer historical research cannot establish this sort of significance for Jesus of Nazareth. It is also clear that the Jesus who is granted this significance is available to contemporary confession—that the historical Jesus is not relegated to the past, but is a once-for-all revelation who gives meaning to the period of preparation, to the time of fulfillment, and above all, to the present. Thus, in a quite different manner, salvation-history theology joins with dialectical theology to participate in the main theological movement of midtwentieth century—the quest of the Christ of faith.

Dialectical Theology
and the Quest of the Christ of Faith

What is the significance of dialectical thought for the theological developments of the 1950s? It promoted the triumph of biblical theology and encouraged the quest of the Christ of faith. This triumph is celebrated in the work of theologians like Reinhold Niebuhr. For all his sociological and psychological insight, Niebuhr was eager to affirm "the biblical view." Niebuhr, of course, was not himself a biblical theologian. The actual task of constructing full-scale biblical theologies was assumed by professional Old and New Testament scholars. Men like Filson and Cullmann explicated complete theologies of the Bible in terms of the history of salvation. Although their work sometimes resembles a systematic theology of the Bible, the intention of these theologians was to present a theology faithful in form and content to the message of the Scriptures. To a degree they were successful, for even the topical arrangement of the theologies of Stauffer and Richardson could be supported by chapter and verse. Because of the importance of the Bible in the Christian tradition, because other theological options seemed inadequate for the times, this new biblical theology became a popular movement. It was taught in the seminaries, proclaimed from the pulpits, and inscribed in the ecumenical documents.

The triumph of biblical theology had been prepared by

dialectical thought. Barth's *Romans* was the call to arms. His intention was to translate the Word of God in the Bible into words which modern man could hear. The word which Barth declared struck a responsive chord in the heart of others who struggled with the crises of the times and searched the Scriptures for an answer. God was the transcendent Lord who had revealed himself in history, and sinful man could receive this redemptive revelation only by faith. In the hands of the dialectical theologians, especially Bultmann, these Pauline-Reformation doctrines were shaped into forms different from the structure of salvation-history theology. Most of all, the dialectical theologians were determined to maintain the basic dialectic—the distinction between God and the world—so that they refused to identify the action of God with particular historical events. They were dedicated to the Reformation's conviction that God remains hidden even in his revelation, that the future remains unseen even in hope. To be sure, Bultmann identified one event—Jesus Christ—with the act of God, but that event, because of its paradoxical nature, was understood as the supreme instance of dialectical revelation.

The more Barth moved in the direction of systematic theology, the more clearly Bultmann emerged as the major biblical theologian of the midtwentieth century. Of all the leading theologians of the day, Bultmann is the only one who remained throughout his career a professional biblical scholar. Because of his devotion to New Testament interpretation, Bultmann has been suspected of reducing the whole theological enterprise to exegesis. "Theology," he says, "is always exegesis inasmuch as it has access to revelation only through the witness of Scripture and seeks to grasp by exegesis what Scripture, understood as witness, says. In form, therefore, theology is always exegesis of Scripture." [41] While this position does not claim the entire theological field for biblical theology, it does assert that the message of the Bible as primary witness to God's revelation has a priority which all theological disciplines should acknowledge.

It can be argued, of course, that Bultmann's theology is not really biblical, and that a salvation-history theologian like Cullmann sets out to make a biblical theology. Yet, the fact that his *Salvation in History* is largely anti-Bultmannian polemic simply shows how Bultmann has dominated the recent scene in biblical thought. To be sure, Bultmann would not, like Niebuhr, talk of the "biblical view," as if the Bible presented a single, unified message. His *Theology of the New Testament* rejects a topical arrangement in favor of an order which stresses the theology of Paul and the theology of John. This arrangement avoids the easy harmonizing which leads to a superficial understanding of the unity of the Bible sometimes apparent in the work of the theologians of *Heilsgeschichte*. They, of course, take the formal structure of the canon more seriously than Bultmann, who adopts a canon within the canon—the Epistles of Paul and the Gospel of John. In his view, even these witnesses to the apostolic message are not to be accepted uncritically. Thus Paul, when he attempts to ground the resurrection in the solid testimony of authentic witness, is charged with betrayal of his own theology. According to Bultmann's critics, judgments like this result from his nonbiblical presuppositions—his loyalty to existentialist methodology. Bultmann's intention, however, is not to impose a philosophical structure upon the Bible, but to employ the method which explicates the Bible's own message. For all his radical criticism, for all his existentialist ontology, Bultmann's entire theological endeavor is devoted to one purpose—to make the basic message of the New Testament clear to modern man.

In any case, the point upon which Barth, the salvation-history theologians, and Bultmann agree is the importance of the Bible and its central message—the witness to Jesus Christ. For all these theologians, the crucial issue is the doctrine of revelation. God has acted in history to disclose his saving purposes, and the supreme event of revelation is Jesus Christ. Bultmann's recognition of the significance of Paul and John rests on a more basic loyalty—his devotion to the early Christian proclamation. Paul and John, and the rest of the New Testament for that matter, are measured against the message of the apostles—the word which testifies to God's Word made flesh. This Word, however, must be proclaimed and heard in our time. Christ cannot remain encased in the museum of Middle Eastern antiquities. He is not there; he is risen—the living Christ who goes before us into every new Galilee. One can find him only by joining in the quest of the Christ of faith.

We can conclude that the biblical theology of midtwentieth century with its focus on the Christ of faith found its most articulate voice in Rudolf Bultmann. To be sure, Bultmann had been inspired and instructed by the Barth of the *Epistle to the Romans*. Yet Barth, for all the breadth and depth of his theological accomplishment, was not able to command the continuing loyalty of most biblical theologians. This was because he could not take with sufficient seriousness what had become basic to practically all biblical scholars—the method of historical criticism. On the other hand, the salvation historians could not produce a biblical theology which was adequate for the times. While their message was couched in biblical language, these theologians lacked a philosophical perspective from which to address contemporary man's most compelling problems. In contrast to both Barth and the salvation-history theologians, Bultmann embraced historical criticism, the universally accepted method, and espoused existentialism, the most relevant philosophy. Thus he provided a climate in which a particular kind of theology could flourish—a theology which was at the same time scientific, relevant, and biblical. From these elements Bultmann developed a comprehensive theological structure which could provide the framework for the quest of the Christ of faith.

Chapter 5

Christ Yesterday and Today

The Theological Synthesis

THE TRIUMPH OF BIBLICAL theology in the middle of the
twentieth century is epitomized by the theological synthesis
of Rudolf Bultmann. That synthesis is composed of elements
central to the theological discussion at the end of the Second
World War: historical criticism, existentialist philosophy,
and dialectical theology. The importance of Bultmann can be
explained by the fact that he was able to mold these three
basic elements into a unified theological model in which every
element worked together for the mutual support of the whole.
Built upon these three foundations, Bultmann's theological
structure provided a framework for the quest of the Christ
of faith. Other biblical theologians labored vigorously under
the shadow of Bultmann's structure, not always happy with
its design, but always building on one or more of its foundations. Their endeavors were strengthened by his demonstra-
tion that the major materials of the day could be built into
a mighty theological fortress. Working toward this end, these

biblical theologians won for biblical theology a central
position in the whole theological enterprise. The purpose of
the present chapter is to investigate and illustrate the nature
and function of the Bultmannian synthesis.

Historically, biblical research flourishes in a climate of
theological synthesis. The prolific scholarship of the Tübingen
school, for example, was fostered by a synthesis of historical-
critical method, idealistic philosophy, and a firm conviction
that the study of Christian origins was relevant for the faith
of nineteenth-century man. That the middle of the twentieth
century was a time of theological synthesis is confirmed by the
massive systematic work of Barth and Tillich. Moreover, the
synthesizing tendency is evident in other biblical theologians
besides Bultmann. The British New Testament scholar E. C.
Hoskyns, for example, combined competence in historical-
critical research with theological sensitivity. His commentary
on the Gospel of John reached beyond the ordinary literary
question to the problem of the meaning of history. Similarly,
Hoskyns's countryman, C. H. Dodd, is well known for his
historical critical work of the Fourth Gospel and his incisive
interpretation of the parables. Yet, Dodd's work was always
inspired by a theological interest and produced such significant contributions to biblical theology as his theory of
realized eschatology and his concept of the kerygma as the
unifying message of the New Testament.

One of the best exemplars of theological synthesis among
American New Testament scholars is John Knox. Informed by
insights from existentialism, dialectical theology and process
thought, Knox was moved by a sincere faith and a serious
commitment to the biblical message and the Christian tradition. Although known for the novelty of his historical-critical

research, Knox is widely recognized as a creative theologian, concerned with such fundamental issues as the nature and interpretation of history. Since God has revealed himself decisively in the event of Christ, history is of ultimate significance, and the Bible, as unique witness to this event, is "absolutely irreplaceable and is of supreme and unique importance." [1] The historical-critical method is valid as the means whereby the historical event can be recovered, but this does not mean that the faith of the Christian is dependent on the results of historical research. Our faith, for example, does not require a reliable biography of Jesus, but demands an encounter with the event of Christ within the community where he is remembered and present. This encounter is possible because Christ and the church constitute a unity wherein the church is understood as an inseparable aspect of the Christ event. As the body of Christ, the Christian community and the reality of the resurrection are one and the same. Thus, in Knox's synthesis, historical criticism and theological insight are enlisted in the quest of the Christ of faith. "In a word," writes Knox, "the whole essential meaning of Christianity is not less, or more, than the meaning of Christ." [2]

Not only did Bultmann work in a climate of theological synthesizing, but an example of theological synthesis had been set before him by his teacher, Wilhelm Herrmann. Herrmann taught systematic theology at Marburg from 1879 to 1917 and influenced a host of students including Karl Barth and Rudolf Bultmann. For Herrmann there is one basic question: What is the essence of faith? His answer embraces a synthesis of nineteenth-century liberalism and the Pauline-Lutheran understanding of revelation and response. Himself an exemplar of liberal theology, Herrmann stood in the line of Schleiermacher and Ritschl. Central to his liberalism was a devotion to the freedom of man—man's right to make his own decision, to believe with integrity. This made Herrmann a foe of orthodoxy in either its Catholic or Protestant form. In waging his antiorthodox crusade, Herrmann was happy to take up the weapons of historical criticism, for these destroyed every effort to defend dogma by historical certainty.

Yet, for all his liberalism, Herrmann maintained an abiding loyalty to the Christian tradition. He believed that faith was not an achievement of man, but a response to God's revelation. "God becomes known to us in no other way," he says, "except that he reveals himself to us." [3] This revelation has occurred for all men in Jesus Christ, yet it is at the same time a disclosure to every concrete individual. This universal-special revelation is not reduced to the Jesus of historical reconstruction, for faith is not dependent on the fallible work of the historian. Instead, faith is man's response to what Herrmann calls "the Christ of history," [4] that is, the Christ of early Christian experience, the Christ to whom the Scriptures bear witness. Although a Christ of faith, this Christ is the fundamental reality of the Jesus of history, namely, the inner life of Jesus. While inaccessible to the historian, Jesus' inner life is factual and discernible to faith. Herrmann's conception of the inner life of Jesus, so severely criticized by his dialectical pupils, made possible a faith grounded in history, yet vital for modern man. In response to God's revelation in the inner life of Jesus, man's own inner life was renewed and brought into communion with God. Therefore, just as Bultmann was able to discern the acts of God in Christ reenacted in the kerygma, so Herrmann was able to discover the religious experience of Jesus reexperienced in the life of the Christian.

The Nature of the Bultmannian Synthesis

Under the inspiration of his teacher, Bultmann has constructed a synthesis of his own. This synthesis, in contrast to the work of many biblical scholars, is comprehensive. Whereas Knox was concerned primarily with Christology and Hoskyns with the problem of history, Bultmann erects a total theological structure. Questions of the ontological ground and methodological basis, only implicit in a scholar like Dodd, are probed to bedrock by Bultmann. This is seen at the outset in his concern to articulate the fundamental theological question—the meaning of existence. The delineaation of the question already discloses the synthetic nature of his theological system, since all three of the major elements in the synthesis converge upon this concern. Historical research into the documents of human history reveals that the question of existence is universal, for every man, consciously or unconsciously, raises the question of the meaning of his own existence. Dialectical theology, too, is concerned with "the decisive question of man in his existence," [5] and considers this question to be identical with the question of God. Existentialist philosophy, because it "offers the most adequate perspective and conceptions for understanding human existence," [6] provides the interpretative tool whereby the question of existence can be explicated. Besides, the Bible, so basic to dialectical theology, is preoccupied with the identical question, for this is what Bultmann means when he asserts that "the philosophers are saying the same thing as the New Testament." [7] Since the Bible and existentialist philosophy are concerned with the same question, "it follows that existentialist philosophy can offer adequate conceptions for the interpretation of the Bible." [8] The synthesis is apparent: the fundamental question of theology is defined by means of historical criticism, existentialist philosophy, and dialectical theology; all three elements of the synthesis raise the identical question—the meaning of existence.

The Negative Function of Historical Criticism

Although the basic question is put in existentialist terms, the answer is provided in Bultmann's theology of the Word. This kerygmatic theology is a biblical or dialectical theology. Since the Bible is the principle witness to the kerygma, the theology of the Word requires biblical interpretation, and the historical-critical method is essential to the interpretation of the Scriptures. Although the method is useful in establishing the biblical text and providing the tools of exegesis, historical criticism within Bultmann's synthesis exercises a largely negative function. It shows what the answer to the fundamental theological question *cannot* be. "I have never yet felt uncomfortable with my critical radicalism," confesses Bultmann, "on the contrary, I have been entirely comfortable. But I often have the impression that my conservative New Testament colleagues feel very uncomfortable, for I see them perpetually engaged in salvage operations. I calmly let the fire burn, for I see that what is consumed is only the fanciful portraits of the Life-of-Jesus theology, and that means nothing other than 'Christ after the flesh.' " [9]

As we have seen, two features of Bultmann's critical research—*Religionsgeschichte* and form criticism—work hand in hand. The *religionsgeschichtliche* method delineates the distinction between the Palestinian and Hellenistic communities and provides the framework for form criticism's designation of the *Sitz-im-Leben* of the various elements of the developing tradition. The history of religions approach, whereby parallels in the religious and cultural environment are investigated, also shows that much of the material which was woven into the Christian tradition was spun on pagan looms. That is, the terms and concepts, myths and symbols which were used to formulate and transmit the tradition were not distinctively Christian. This raises the question about the uniqueness of early Christianity. Moreover, since the thought forms of early Christianity belong to an ancient, foreign world, the relevance of the biblical message for modern man was put in question.

The results of form criticism were still more negative. Whereas nineteenth-century theology found the basis of faith in the life of Jesus, form criticism demonstrated that a reliable biography could not be produced. Consequently, the effort to go behind the doctrine of the early church to discover the real Jesus of Nazareth was frustrated. The earliest witnesses to Jesus already had seen him through the eyes of faith, and their first testimony to his words and deeds hailed him as risen Lord. The Christ of faith, not the historical Jesus, was the central concern of the New Testament message. To be sure, the historian could find some shreds of authentic tradition, and from these erect a fragmentary image of the man from Nazareth. A vital faith, however, could hardly be built on so frail a foundation, constructed by the fallible procedures of human research. Form criticism, together with the history of religions method, had produced two negative results:

1. It is impossible to base faith on the Jesus of historical reconstruction.
2. It is impossible to base faith on the New Testament form of the proclamation of Christ.

The first of these conclusions derailed the quest of the historical Jesus; the second denounced the search for a biblical creed. What seems to have been demanded was another understanding of the kerygma and a different conception of faith.

The Kerygma in Existentialist Reinterpretation

The historical criticism which undercut the false kerygma also cleared the ground for the growth of the true. The true kerygmatic theology (see chapter 4), which is rooted in Paul and cultivated by Luther, flourishes in the dialectical thought of the twentieth century. This theology stresses the holiness of God and the sinfulness of man, and claims that knowledge of God can come only by divine revelation. That revelation has occurred in Jesus Christ—the act of God in history, the event of judgment and redemption. For the man who stands at a distance from the original happening, the event of revelation recurs in the proclamation of the Word. Man receives this redemptive revelation by faith, by the risk of his old securities, by taking up the cross to be crucified with Christ.

Reading this brief summary of Bultmannian theology, one can understand why Karl Jaspers accuses Bultmann of a "frozen orthodoxy." [10] Yet, while it may seem to reflect first-century Rome or sixteenth-century Wittenberg, it is in Bultmann's understanding neither frozen nor orthodox. For this sort of theology to have meaning, it must be interpreted, or we may say, reinterpreted. The ground for that reinterpretation is to be found in the fundamental theological dialectic—

the infinite qualitative difference between time and eternity. The fact that this dialectic was formulated by Kierkegaard, the father of existentialism, and transmitted by Barth, the father of dialectical theology, indicates, as we have observed, that a close relationship exists between existentialism and dialectical theology. As a matter of fact, this basic dialectic provides the ontological ground for Bultmann's theological synthesis. This common ontological ground becomes the basis for Bultmann's use of existentialist analysis in the explication of dialectical theology. Consequently, in response to Barth's criticism of his use of existentialist philosophy, Bultmann can reply that he has employed existentialism merely as a means to establish and clarify methodologically the original theological impulse stated in the preface to the second edition of Barth's *Romans*. The method, however, has shaped the theology. And, while Bultmann may be more consistently loyal to the original dialectic, Barth is correct in noting that Bultmann's theology, while indebted to Luther, is not identical with the thought of Paul and the reformers. In the light of existentialist philosophy, Bultmann has reinterpreted the teachings of Paul, Luther, and Karl Barth.

The character of Bultmann's thought as existentialist reinterpretation of the theology of the Word is clarified as one considers what Bultmann means by the doctrines he affirms. We have seen, for example, that he stresses the holiness of God and the sinfulness of man. Although this is the same God whom Luther describes as the hidden God and Barth as the wholly other, Bultmann, while able to use these terms, is inclined to interpret God in existentialist language. For instance, he is fond of talking about God as the God of the future—the God whose "transcendence is . . . his constant futurity, his absolute freedom." [11] God is defined in terms of the possibility of existence which is always coming to man in the decisions man continues to face in history.

Similar insights emerge from an analysis of Bultmann's idea of man. Although he agrees with Barth and the reformers that man is a sinner, Bultmann understands man and his sin in terms of existentialist anthropology. For Bultmann, sin is inauthentic existence. Man as sinner has lost his freedom and become submerged in the world, trying to grasp for security in what Heidegger would call "the things at hand." In describing man before faith, Bultmann essentially follows existentialist anthropology: man is a being with a relation to himself who can decide about his own existence, who makes the wrong decision and forfeits the freedom which belongs to his original being. Yet, while this analysis of man's existence is indebted to Heidegger, Bultmann is able by careful philological and exegetical research to argue that the same understanding of man underlies the anthropological language of Paul.

A similar interdependent functioning of the elements of the Bultmannian synthesis can be seen in Bultmann's understanding of Christ. As the exegesis of 2 Corinthians 5:16 demonstrates, the Christian is no longer preoccupied with the Christ after the flesh. Besides, historical criticism has shown that this Christ—the historical Jesus—cannot be reconstructed, while the existential dialectic has insisted that an objective ground for faith is impossible. This means that the Christ of faith—the Christ of the kerygma—is the concern of the believer. It does not mean, however, that the man of faith must give assent to the ancient formulas of the kerygma or the christological creeds of the New Testament. As the history of religions method shows, these creeds and formulas use the signs and symbols of the Hellenistic world and are not distinctively Christian. These signs and symbols, therefore, must not be taken as literal descriptions of the nature of Christ. They must be interpreted by means of historical-existentialist exegesis to make clear their true intention—their confession of the meaning of God's action in Christ for man's existence. As God's action for man's existence, Christ is not confined to the past; the crucified one is also the risen Lord. The resurrection, however, is not an objective miracle of divine intervention into history, but an eschatological, indeed, an existential event. It is the event of *"faith in the saving efficacy of the cross"* [12]—an event in the existence of the believer.

Just as Bultmann's understanding of Christ reveals the complex interrelation of the elements of his synthesis, so also does his idea of the word. By historical criticism, Bultmann indicates that the proper background for interpreting the word is biblical—the idea of the dynamic Word of God spoken by the Old Testament prophets. Moreover, once the form critic has dug through the layers of later tradition, he discovers the Jesus of the earliest historical level as a prophet who announced the imminence of the kingdom of God. This historical Jesus is, for Bultmann, the "bearer of the word." By means of his understanding of the word, Bultmann is able to detect a line of continuity between the historical Jesus and the Christ of the church's kerygma. Both Jesus and the church declare the dynamic Word of God which calls for radical obedience. But, whereas Jesus announced an event of the imminent future, the church proclaimed an event of the immediate past. In the preaching of the church, the proclaimer had become the proclaimed—the eschatological event of Jesus' expectation had been fulfilled in the death-resurrection of Christ. The fact that the church proclaimed

an event of the past, however, does not mean that the Word is
a bare recital of historical happenings. Instead, the kerygma
is itself a dynamic event—an eschatological or existential
event through which the act of God in Christ confronts man in
the present with the decision of faith. In response to this Word,
man is able to receive salvation, that is, he is able, in Bultmann's words, to "understand myself and my situation in
terms of the word." [13] Salvation means self-understanding,
authentic existence, freedom for the future, in short, the
salvation which the existentialist philosopher seeks but is
unable to find.

Man's response to the word of salvation is faith. In expli-
cating the meaning of faith, all three of the elements of
Bultmann's synthesis again come into play. Historical criticism indicates that John did not understand faith as affirmation of his reconstruction of the life of Jesus, and that Paul
did not conceive of faith as assent to his formulation of the
kerygma. Besides, historical criticism has shown that a
reliable reconstruction of the historical Jesus is impossible
and that the Pauline structure of the kerygma was patterned
after pagan models. Existentialism, at the same time, has
argued that faith cannot have an objective ground—that the
dialectic between God and man cannot be spanned by a
bridge built by man from the materials of the world. Instead,
faith means quitting all building, abandoning the world's
materials. It means absolute risk, a leap into the void. This
is the faith which Barth, Luther, and Paul are confessing,
too—a faith made possible not by man's effort, but God's
grace, so that even man's faith is understood as God's gift.
This gift, nevertheless, belongs to the existence of man, for
he is the kind of being who can decide—a being who, though
trapped in the inevitability of sin, retains his basic respon-

sibility. Thus, faith is man's decision, the existential possibility through which he gains authentic self-understanding. "So it is," says Bultmann, "that faith is the new possibility for existence before God; it is created by God's saving act, is laid hold of in obedience, and manifests itself as confession and hope, as fear and trust—in short, as a new understanding of oneself." [14]

What is the meaning of all of this? Basically, Bultmann has taken the fundamental doctrines of dialectical theology—the legacy of Paul and Luther—and by means of historical criticism and existentialist analysis interpreted them to meet the needs of his time. Historical criticism has dismantled the old structure—nineteenth-century liberalism and the last vestiges of Lutheran orthodoxy. Existentialism has provided the key which liberates the vital faith of the biblical witness and the Protestant Reformation—the message proclaimed by the dialectical theologians. The result is an impressive theological position with compelling power to synthesize the major interests of the midtwentieth century, a theology which is scientifically sound, biblically based, and relevant to man's existence. Bultmann's thought is a special kind of biblical theology which answers the problem of human existence in terms of God's revelation. This revelation has occurred in history in Jesus Christ, but it must recur in the existence of the man of faith. This recurrence takes place in the preaching of the Word, ancient and modern, in which the Jesus of history is proclaimed as the Christ of faith.

Synthesis at Work: Demythologizing

"This method of interpretation of the New Testament which tries to recover the deeper meaning behind the

mythological conceptions," says Bultmann, "I call demythologizing." [15] This explication requires at the outset an
understanding of Bultmann's idea of myth. Failure to begin
here has led to considerable misunderstanding within the
demythologizing debate. For Bultmann, the basic definition
is relatively clear. "Mythology," he writes, "is the use of
imagery to express the other worldly in terms of this world
and the divine in terms of human life, the other side in terms
of this side." [16] Or again, "It may be said that myths give
to the transcendent reality an immanent, this-worldly
objectivity. Myths give worldly objectivity to that which is
unworldly." [17]

Although Bultmann claims that this definition has been
learned from the history of religions school, it is clear that
his basic theological dialectic is involved—the dialectic of
eternity and time, the transcendent and the immanent, the
other world and this world. In other words, the fundamental
Bultmannian dialectic which serves as the ontological ground
for his theological synthesis is already assumed in his definition. This is apparent in the further explication of Bultmann's
idea of myth. The activities of the gods, for example, are
described like activities of men, and natural happenings,
such as storms and earthquakes, are attributed to transcendent causes, the work of spirits and demons. This attempt to
depict transcendent powers in the imagery of the world, to
objectify the essentially nonobjective, results in a cosmology
which presents the world as a three-story building with
heaven upstairs, the earth on the ground floor, and the under-
world in the basement.

This world view, which obviously violates the fundamental
distinction between time and eternity, enshrines a deeper
truth—ancient man's understanding of existence. Conse-

quently, the real intention of myth is not to relate entertaining stories about the gods nor to provide fanciful explanations for natural or historical phenomena, but to bring into vivid expression man's own understanding of himself. "The real purpose of myth," says Bultmann, "is not to present an objective picture of the world as it is, but to express man's understanding of himself in the world in which he lives." [18] Or again, "Mythology expresses a certain understanding of human existence. It believes that the world and human life have their ground and their limits in a power which is beyond all that we can calculate or control. Mythology speaks about this power inadequately and insufficiently because it speaks about it as if it were a worldly power." [19] All of this makes it evident that myth has a positive as well as a negative side. The negative side is that myth erroneously expresses the transcendent in objective or cosmic terms; the positive, that myth expresses truth about man's existence. In terms of the Bultmannian synthesis, myth, defined according to the history of religions school, blurs the basic existentialist-theological dialectic.

Why must we demythologize? The answer is implicit in Bultmann's definition. We must search behind the false objectifying to discover the meaning of existence the myth intends to express. However, in giving his reason, Bultmann notes that modern man is unable to accept the mythological world view. For modern man, steeped in the scientific concept of an ordered universe of cause and effect, the notion of a three-storied world where spiritual forces change the weather or the stability of the earth is simply incredible. The demand that man should believe such nonsensical remnants of antiquity is in effect a demand for a *sacrificium intellectus* and is therefore a denial of man's basic existence. It also contradicts Bultmann's understanding of faith as responsible decision. But along with his existentialism and his idea of faith, Bultmann's liberalism has played a major role here. The demand for freedom and intellectual integrity in faith is a nineteeth-century dictum which Bultmann had learned from Wilhelm Herrmann. With the liberals of the nineteenth century, Bultmann finds it impossible to believe in the historicity of the nature miracles and the physical resurrection.

Just as his liberalism and his existentialism call for demythologizing, so also does Bultmann's dialectical theology. This is seen in his appeal to Paul and John as providing the precedent for his program. Since these authors of the New Testament demythologize the eschatology of the Bible, Bultmann is given biblical authority to proceed with demythologizing. Because "de-mythologizing has its beginning in the New Testament itself," says Bultmann, "our task of de-mythologizing today is justified." [20] This seems to suggest that, in spite of the cosmological concerns of some sections of the Bible, the New Testament at its best is really interested in the meaning of human existence. "Hence," Bultmann can say, "the importance of the New Testament mythology lies not in its imagery but in the understanding of existence which it enshrines." [21]

In a deeper sense, Bultmann is claiming that the kerygma itself demands demythologization. The kerygma is in essence nonobjective—a dynamic event which announces God's saving act. Faith in the kerygma has no objective ground; faith is rather acceptance of God's act in radical risk. Thus, if one should suppose that his faith hangs on the question of whether Jesus walked on the water or not, or whether Christ was pre-existent or not, he is not considering the question of faith in the kerygma at all. Instead, he is transforming the kerygma into myth—turning the transcendent into the this-worldly by misconstruing the miracles as facts and the Gnostic myth as dogma.

Demythologizing, by way of contrast, shows what the kerygma really demands, what faith really is. At the center of the kerygma stands the cross of Christ—the scandal of the gospel which confronts man and calls him to radical obedience. The decision of faith must be made in response to this stark reality, and not to mythological distortions of it. "The purpose of demythologizing," writes Bultmann, "is not to make religion more acceptable to modern man by trimming the traditional Biblical texts, but to make clearer to modern man what the Christian faith is. He must be confronted with the issue of decision, be provoked to decision by the fact that the stumbling block to faith, the *skandalon*, is peculiarly disturbing to man in general, not only to modern man. . . . Therefore my attempt to demythologize begins, true enough, by clearing away the false stumbling-blocks created for modern man by the fact that his world-view is determined by science." [22] Why demythologize? Historical criticism (performing its negative function), existentialism (providing the means for existential understanding), and dialectical theology (defining the character of the kerygma and faith) demand it.

What is the nature of Bultmann's program of demythologizing? In general, it is his whole theological endeavor which we have been discussing, and, more precisely, it is the application of his hermeneutic to the task of interpreting the New Testament texts. The title "demythologizing" is, by Bultmann's own admission, "an unsatisfactory word." [23] It is unsatisfactory because it can lead to the mistaken notion

that Bultmann intends to eliminate the mythological elements
from the New Testament message. Bultmann has never published a demythologized edition of the New Testament, dras-
tically cut down to fit the pocket of modern man. The aim of
demythologizing, he says, "is not to eliminate the mythological statements but to interpret them." [24]

Actually, demythologizing, as Erich Dinkler has pointed
out, is "existentialist interpretation of the New Testament." [25]
Two questions, however, can be raised in regard to the procedure and practice of demythologizing: 1) Does Bultmann
really interpret and not eliminate the myth? 2) Does Bultmann in the process of demythologizing actually remytholo-
gize the New Testament message?

In regard to the first question, there can be no doubt that
Bultmann intends to interpret and not to eliminate the myth.
Nevertheless, a lack of clarity concerning the original intention of the New Testament writers, together with the correlative function of liberalism and existentialism within the
demythologizing process, appears to qualify this intention.
By means of existentialist analysis, Bultmann interprets the
meaning of myth for man's existence. This interpretation is
legitimized by the New Testament itself which, according to
Bultmann, intends to present in mythological form an understanding of human existence. The writers of the New Testament, however, not only use myth as a means to express their
understanding of existence, they actually posit a world view
which they hold to be valid. The resulting shift from anthropology to cosmology, in Bultmann's view, distorts the New
Testament understanding of man's existence. Insofar as
myth expresses cosmological concepts it should be eliminated,
and the process of elimination is carried out by liberalism's
historical method.

In this process, Bultmann seems to assume the superiority of the modern world view over the ancient, and to use the former as a criterion for evaluating the latter. In light of the scientific recognition of natural law, Bultmann says, for example, that "the *idea of miracle* has . . . become untenable and *it must be abandoned*." [26] To be sure, Bultmann retains the idea of *wonder* (see chapter 4)—an event through which God acts for man's redemption, perceived by the eyes of faith. It is also true that Bultmann is able to interpret the miracles existentially as expressing the New Testament's idea of the transcendence of God or the Lordship of Christ. Nevertheless, the biblical miracles insofar as they represent cosmic or historical happenings are, by means of historical criticism, virtually eliminated.

In regard to the second question, we may ask: If Bultmann has used the scientific world view as a means for evaluating New Testament cosmology, is it not true that he has simply exchanged the old world view for the new? And, if the liberal Bultmann prefers a more up-to-date explanation of natural phenomena, is it not true that he has adopted the nineteenth-century world view—one which is now outmoded and hence "mythological"? In short, is it not true that Bultmann has not demythologized, but remythologized the New Testament message? Bultmann is quick to point out that the scientific view of the world can in no sense be described as mythological. It does not attribute natural and historical happenings to the intervention of spiritual or demonic powers. Science, in either its nineteenth-century or most recent form, has to accept such concepts as cause and effect and the order of nature before it lights a Bunsen burner. Implicit here is Bultmann's obvious preference for the scientific method as a means to understand natural phenomena, along with a depre-

catory assessment of the mythological world view—factors
which simply bring into focus the importance of liberalism
for Bultmann's theological synthesis.

It is a mistake, however, to characterize Bultmann's
demythologizing as essentially a shift from one world view
to another, in spite of the debt his liberalism owes to the
scientific perspective. Bultmann is ardently opposed to the
objectifying or absolutizing of any world view, ancient or
modern. Although this opposition reflects a form of liberalism
which refuses to be enslaved by any historical formulation of
truth, it rests at its deepest level on Bultmann's fundamental
existentialist-theological dialectic—a dialectic which sees
any attempt to objectify the transcendent to be the unpardon-
able theological sin. Consequently, at the conclusion of his
most complete presentation of demythologizing, Bultmann
can paraphrase 1 Corinthians 7:29–31 to read, "Let those
who have the modern world-view live as though they had
none." [27] Indeed, Bultmann's objection to the scientific world
view is its tendency to objectification; he wrote to Karl Barth,
"The 'myth of the 20th century' is a perverted myth. Thus,
if the true myth is the making this-worldly of the transcendent, the myth of the 20th century is the making transcendent
(the absolutizing) of the this-wordly." [28] The answer to our
second question, whether Bultmann in the process of demythologizing actually remythologizes the New Testament message,
is a clear-cut No!

Demythologizing as a method of theological synthesis is
well expressed by Bultmann's statement that "our radical
attempt to demythologize the New Testament is in fact a
perfect parallel to Paul and Luther's doctrine of justification
by faith alone apart from the works of the Law, or rather, it
carries this doctrine to its logical conclusion in the field of
epistemology." [29] This means that just as man, according to

Paul and Luther, could not justify himself by moral works, so he cannot, according to Bultmann, establish his theological position by works of the mind. All three elements in Bultmann's synthesis come into focus for the elucidation of this unifying theme. Historical criticism has shown that man cannot by historical works reconstruct a solid ground for faith. Existentialist philosophy has shown that faith is authentic self-understanding; it is personal and individual, without external verification. Dialectical theology has shown that faith is radical risk; it accepts God's eschatological act without props and propositions. In this final coalescence of the Bultmannian synthesis, the Pauline-Lutheran idea of faith is interpreted by existentialist analysis as authentic self-understanding, and authentic self-understanding is identified with the Pauline-Lutheran idea of faith.

Although it is the focal point of Bultmann's theological work, demythologizing has two major limitations. First, the idea of *God as acting* is not a mythological concept. Bultmann's opponents have sometimes charged that his program of demythologization has not been carried through to its logical conclusion, since he retains the idea of God as acting. This idea, though buried in sophisticated theological verbiage, appears to involve the notion that God has intervened in history and seems little removed from the mythological beliefs of ancient man. The objection, however, fails to understand what Bultmann means by the act of God (see chapter 3). For him, it is not a miraculous action distinct from the events of history, but an action in and through them. The act of God is an eschatological or existential event. In it the transcendent is not objectified or remythologized, for, as Bultmann says, "When we speak of God as acting, we do not speak mythologically in the objectifying sense." [30]

The fact, however, that the act of God is a nonobjective,

existential event does not mean that it is a subjective or
unreal event—a subjective appropriation of a timeless truth.
The act of God is always *existentiell* happening, always
occurring in the concrete, particular situation of man. To be
sure, the God who acts cannot be described in metaphysical
terms, for that would involve a remythologizing or objectifying of the transcendent. God can only be described in analogical terms, and although this involves a type of imagery,
analogy is not a mythological expression. The concepts used,
especially the idea of God as Father, do not represent a
remythologizing, but speak to the existential reality of man's
being. Moreover, the fact that God cannot be known apart
from man's existence does not mean that God does not exist
apart from man. The act of God for man's salvation, therefore, is an action from the outside; it is not a mythological
concept; it cannot be demythologized.

Demythologizing is also limited by a second closely related
factor. The action of God, essential to man's salvation, is
uniquely related to the *historical Jesus*. "Jesus," says Bultmann, "is a human, historical person from Nazareth in
Galilee. His work and destiny happened within world-history
and as such come under the scrutiny of the historian who can
understand them as part of the nexus of history." [31] It is
through this particular historical event that God has acted
once for the salvation of all men. In face of the liberal
challenge that he ought to abandon this last remnant of early
Christian mythology, and in response to the philosophical
charge that his insistence on the necessity of Jesus involves a
contradiction of his existentialist ontology, Bultmann continues to hold on to the *Dass*—the sheer historicity of Jesus
as essential to salvation (see chapter 4). Bultmann stolidly
refuses to allow his gospel to be dekerygmatized.

In holding on to this historical absolute, Bultmann creates problems for his theological synthesis. On the one hand, his radical use of historical criticism seems to be compromised, since the historicity of Jesus is surely subject to the proof or disproof of the historian. On the other hand, his identification of the historical Jesus as the unique saving act of God appears to violate his basic dialectic, to involve the objectifying of the transcendent. To be sure, Bultmann does not allow the details of the life of Jesus—the historical reconstruction— to become the ground of faith, and he does interpret the sheer historical event existentially as eschatological occurrence. Bultmann's basic answer to these problems, however, is articulated in terms of the event itself. At the center of the event stands the cross of Christ, and under the shadow of this cross the event is seen to be so scandalous in nature that it defies every effort at historical proof or philosophical explanation. It demands a faith as radical risk—a faith dialectical in its very essence.

An intriguing question remains to be answered: Does one element in the Bultmannian synthesis predominate? Is Bultmann, most of all, a liberal, an existentialist, or a dialectical theologian? The appropriate response is that Bultmann fits none of these categories exactly, but should be characterized according to the unique synthesis he has developed. The difficulty of classification is underscored by Karl Barth, who was not entirely content with his own assessment of Bultmann as "simply a Lutheran" of a special sort.[32] Nevertheless, it can be concluded that within the structure one fundamental element bears more weight than the other two. For most interpreters, this is the element of existentialist philosophy. This conclusion can be supported by the observation that existentialist analysis has been decisive in formulating the basic theological question, and by the fact that existentialist anthropology has played a major role in interpreting Bultmann's central doctrines.

On the other hand, it can be argued that liberalism is the predominant element. Support for this case can be found in Bultmann's allegiance to the freedom of faith and his devotion to the scientific method—a method which is able at points to eliminate myth at the expense of existentialist interpretation.

Two factors, however, demonstrate that dialectical theology and not existentialism or liberalism is the most important feature of the Bultmannian synthesis. The first is Bultmann's insistence that salvation cannot be attained by man apart from God's action. As we have seen (in chapter 3), Bultmann, while accepting the existentialist diagnosis of man's predicament, cannot prescribe existentialism's remedy. Redemption can only come from outside, from God's grace, God's revelation.

The second factor is Bultmann's conviction that God's saving action occurs uniquely and absolutely in the historical Jesus (see chapter 4). In the face of charges of inconsistency and frozen orthodoxy, Bultmann remains adamant in his dedication to the *Dass*—the sheer fact *that* God acted decisively in Jesus. These two factors cannot be reduced to existentialist subjectivity. They defy demythologization and they declare that Bultmann is a biblical theologian who stands in the tradition of Luther and Paul. Far from being a foe of biblical theology, Bultmann has been one of its most ardent advocates throughout the first half of the twentieth century. All of his theological effort has been enlisted in the search for the fundamental message of the Bible, the quest of the Christ of faith.

Chapter 6

Christ Passing
through the Midst of Them

The Dissolution of the Theological Synthesis

RUDOLF BULTMANN HAS BUILT his theological structure on three foundations—historical criticism, existentialist philosophy, and dialectical theology—which have also supported a variety of biblical theologies. But now the foundations have begun to tremble and the walls to crack.

The present has been dubbed the post-Bultmann era, the time of crisis in biblical theology. The place of the Bible in theological construction and the importance of historical revelation for the theological blueprint have been overshadowed by the skyscrapers of our secular cities. What has befallen Bultmann's towering edifice? Why has the movement of biblical theology and the quest of the Christ of faith run into a stone wall? In answer to these questions, this chapter will attempt to show that the Bultmannian structure has toppled not only because of tensions between the elements of his synthesis but because of shifts within the foundational elements. The latter point not only creates problems for

119

Bultmann, it also challenges other biblical theologians whose work rests upon the same foundations. At the same time, the decline of Bultmann and the debility of biblical theology have raised questions concerning the possibility and legitimacy of the quest of the Christ of faith.

Tensions within the Bultmannian Synthesis

Historical Criticism and Existentialist Philosophy

Within the theological system of Rudolf Bultmann, a tension exists between historical criticism and existentialist philosophy. We have just observed that Bultmann employs both of these elements as correlative methods in his theological enterprise. Historical criticism has been used to show that the quest of the historical Jesus is virtually impossible, that the Jesus proclaimed by the earliest Christians was the Christ of faith. Existentialist philosophy, on the other hand, has been employed to demonstrate that the quest of the historical Jesus is illegitimate, that a Jesus established by historical research is an improper object for faith. Working together, the two methods indicate that the Christ of the early Christian kerygma is the Christ who confronts the modern believer with the decision about his existence. The Christ of the New Testament and the Christ of Rudolf Bultmann are one and the same.

Yet, although the two methods may have worked together for the good of those who love the Lord, the question can be raised: Do the methods of historical criticism and existentialist philosophy work together consistently? The former represents a procedure whereby tools borrowed from the natural sciences are applied to the study of history. The method is objective, empirical, and rational. Its object, as nineteenth-century historians like von Ranke made clear, is to discern the bare facts. The existentialist method, by way of contrast, does not focus on objective happenings, but on the significance of historical events for man's existence. The historian, far from being coldly objective in regard to the empirical data, must recognize himself to be a participant in the history he interprets. Moreover, what he attempts to interpret is not the course or outcome of history, but himself. For the existentialist historian, the concern of historical understanding is self-understanding.

Bultmann seems to be aware of the fact that his adoption of the existentialist method qualifies his use of historical criticism. One of his earliest writings, for example, notes that "the essence of history cannot be grasped by 'viewing' it, as we view our natural environment" since "our relationship to history is wholly different from our relationship to nature."[1] In similar fashion Bultmann is fond of faulting the Greek way of considering man and history according to the analogy of nature. The Greeks, in his judgment, wrongly see man as a part of the cosmos and view history as a cosmic process. For them, "we can say that the task of historiography was understood from analogy with the task of natural science."[2] Yet, this Greek perspective, which looms up in Bultmann's imagination like some awesome pagan idol, seems to be similar to the understanding of history presupposed by nineteenth-century historical criticism—the view that history can be understood in the same way as nature.

However, if history cannot be understood in the same way as nature, how is Bultmann justified in using historical criticism at all? Rather than answering the question explicitly, Bultmann seems merely to assume the necessity of the historical-critical approach. Thus he says, "The one presupposition that cannot be dismissed is *the historical method* of interrogating the text." [3] The implicit answer, however, must be that Bultmann, for all his concern with the meaning of history, continues his interest in objective historical happenings. It is through the events of objective history that God acts, even though the acts of God are not identical with the historical events. Through the eyes of faith, the *geschichtlich* events are perceived to occur within the *historisch* happenings.

This might seem to suggest that Bultmann is adopting one method, historical criticism for *Historie*, and another, existentialist interpretation, for *Geschichte*, as though one could change rules when playing a different hand. Such a simple solution is impossible, however, since the *geschichtlich* event occurs through the *historisch*, so that the two cannot be separated. Besides, the historian is unavoidably involved as existential participant in history regardless of the method employed in his research. Yet, the two methods, historical criticism and existentialist interpretation, are used together in a fashion which is far from clear. As Heinrich Ott points out, Bultmann has not adequately answered the question, "How is it that historical reality is accessible partly to objectivizing observation and partly to existential experience?" [4] In the resulting hybrid, Bultmann claims that the "most subjective" interpretation has become the "most objective," [5] but in the process, the distinction between objective and subjective appears to have been badly blurred.

This confusion in the use of the historical criticism and existentialist interpretation rests ultimately on differing views of historical reality presupposed by the two methods—a point illustrated by Bultmann's understanding of the resurrection. For him, the resurrection is not an objective happening which could have been photographed by a reporter from the Galilean Gazette; rather it is an existential event. The resurrection did not take place in the garden tomb of old Jerusalem, but in the heart of the believer. The resurrection is the event whereby the man of faith embraces the cross as God's action for his salvation.

Far from implying a denial of the reality of the resurrection, as some critics have charged, this understanding of the resurrection, given Bultmann's existentialism, intends to underscore its reality. For Bultmann, existential events are the most "real." Nevertheless, this conclusion serves to show that a different concept of reality is involved—a concept which is quite beyond the grasp of historical criticism. The reality presupposed by that method is grounded in the naturalistic positivism of the nineteenth century, whereas Bultmann's understanding rests on an existentialist ontology which is basically opposed to it. In short, Bultmann's two methods assume varying views of reality which stand in fundamental conflict.

Existentialism and Dialectical Theology

Bultmann's theology also displays a tension between existentialism and dialectical theology. As we have seen (in chapter 4), the content of Bultmann's thought reflects the theological image of the early Karl Barth. The features of this theological portrait include the idea of holy God and human sinner, and the doctrine of salvation by faith in God's revelation in Jesus Christ. In Bultmann's vision, however, this image is filtered through the prism of existentialist philosophy, with the result that theology becomes anthropology and Christology soteriology. This reinterpretation of basic biblical doctrines in terms of existentialism has engen-

dered the charge that Bultmann has reduced the message of
the Scriptures to a bare theological minimum, and is guilty
of a "great reduction." [6] For example, biblical eschatology
with its vision of the future fulfillment of God's long drama
of redemption finds its meaning in the present moment of
the believer's decision. The biblical idea of creation, involving a cosmic purpose, is dismissed as Hellenistic mythology
and swallowed up into the subjective experience of the new
creation.

To be sure, Bultmann applies the brakes to this existentialist runaway at two points: first, his insistence that
salvation cannot come from human acquisition or self-
understanding, but from outside, from an act of God; second,
his conviction that God's saving action can be specifically and
exclusively identified with the historical Jesus (see chapter 4).
Both of these points represent features of biblical theology
which defy demythologization. The second point—Bultmann's
identification of God's saving action with the historical
Jesus—seems, however, to disturb the basic existentialist
dialectic. Along with the early Barth, Bultmann has embraced
Kierkegaard's idea of the infinite qualitative distinction
between time and eternity, the idea that a great gulf has been
fixed between man and God. This dialectic has provided the
ground for the claim, basic to demythologizing, that the transcendent should not be objectified. Yet, the identification of
God's saving action with a particular event of history appears
to imply some objectification of the divine act. Bultmann,
to be sure, maintains that God only acts *through* the *historisch*
event; the event of revelation is itself dialectical, and God
remains hidden even in his revelation. Nevertheless, Bultmann's absolutizing of the *Dass*—the fact *that* God acted in
Jesus—does put considerable stress on the durability of the

dialectic. His insistence that God's saving action in Jesus cannot be demythologized merely serves to show that existentialist interpretation has its limitations, or, in other words, that Bultmann has compromised his existentialism through his loyalty to Pauline-Reformation theology.

From a slightly different perspective, Schubert Ogden has scored Bultmann's failure to maintain his existentialist ontology consistently.[7] According to Ogden, Bultmann's devotion to the decisive character of God's redemptive action in Jesus constitutes a "structural inconsistency" in Bultmann's position. This inconsistency becomes apparent when one reduces the Bultmannian position to two elementary propositions.

1. According to Bultmann's existentialist anthropology, the possibility of authentic existence is available to every man.

2. According to Bultmann's theological conclusion, authentic existence is actually realized only through commitment to God's action in the historical Jesus.

In short, what Bultmann holds to be a possibility in principle turns out to be an impossibility in fact.

Not everyone, of course, accepts Ogden's interpretation of Bultmann, and there can be little doubt that Ogden construes the entire Bultmannian system in terms of existentialist ontology, and views Bultmann primarily as a philosopher. As we have seen (in chapter 5), Bultmann is more appropriately to be evaluated as a biblical theologian, devoted to the Pauline-Lutheran understanding of the Word. Consequently, Bultmann's own response to the criticism is to claim that what Ogden calls a contradiction is in truth the basic *skandalon* of the Christian faith—that God's action for man's salvation occurs in this particular one, this crucified Christ.[8] Nevertheless, this line of defense only serves to underscore the point under consideration: Bultmann's existentialism and his biblical or dialectical theology stand in tension. To assert that the Pauline paradox is an answer to his philosophical inconsistency simply says that Bultmann is ready to purchase the biblical faith at the expense of the existentialist ontology he elsewhere adopts.

Dialectical Theology and Historical Criticism

Finally, there is tension between Bultmann's dialectical theology and his historical criticism. As we have seen, Bultmann borrows the method of nineteenth-century liberalism and, as a radical critic, dismisses such matters as the nature miracles and the physical resurrection with a slight flourish of the pen. On the other hand, he clings to a biblical theology which stresses the necessity of God's saving action in Jesus Christ with all the fervor of an evangelist. As Langdon Gilkey observes, the theology of the 1950s "is half liberal and modern . . . and half biblical and orthodox." [9] Bultmann, of course, is no Billy Graham, and there can be little doubt that he continues to suffer from a liberal hangover. His assessment of the first-century world view is a case in point.

Although Bultmann's avowed intention is to interpret rather than eliminate the biblical myths (see chapter 5), he easily dispenses with the three-storied universe as a useless product of primitive cosmology. The idea that heaven is above, of course, can be shown by existentialist interpretation to symbolize God's transcendence. Yet, how are we to deny that the biblical writers took their cosmology seriously, that they really believed heaven was "up there," that biblical cosmology *is* an aspect of biblical theology? Bultmann's claim that acceptance of the biblical world view constitutes a sacrifice of the intellect merely indicates that the modern scientific world view has become the criterion for evaluating the ancient, that biblical mythology, insofar as cosmic matters are concerned, is virtually eliminated. In terms of the present discussion, Bultmann's biblical theology is compromised by his nineteenth-century liberalism.

The clearest evidence of the tension between dialectical theology and historical criticism, however, is to be detected in Bultmann's understanding of the kerygma. His view, of course, is further removed from C. H. Dodd's perspective than the distance across the English Channel. For Dodd, the kerygma is a pattern of facts or doctrines about Jesus Christ —a sort of formula which recurs throughout the New Testament documents. For Bultmann, on the other hand, the kerygma is a dynamic, nonobjective event—the proclamation of Christ who encounters man and calls him to radical faith. While Bultmann believes he is able to derive this understanding of the kerygma from the New Testament by means of historical criticism, there can be little doubt that his results are determined by dialectical theology's idea of the Word. Moreover, this dynamic understanding of the proclamation enables Bultmann to put the kerygma out of reach of the historical critics. Since the kerygma is a nonobjective event— the proclaiming of the Christ of faith—it escapes the scrutiny of historical criticism which can neither affirm nor deny its essential truth. Like Wilhelm Herrmann's "inner life of Jesus," Bultmann's kerygma seems invulnerable to historical attack. Bultmann, in other words, utilizes his theology of the Word to overcome the limits of his liberalism.

This theology of the Word has also allowed a conception of theological continuity whereby a unity of the New Testament message could be affirmed. Although historical criticism had demonstrated the discontinuity between Jesus and the Hellenistic church, the theology of the kerygma has posited a continuity wherein Jesus is viewed as the bearer of the Word and Paul as the proclaimer of the Word. Thus Bultmann's historical criticism and his dialectical theology are in conflict on the question of the continuity of the basic biblical message.

The problem is compounded, however, when Bultmann proceeds to insist that the saving kerygma is uniquely related to the action of God in the Jesus of history. In so far as the kerygma is dependent on that particular *historisch* event, it does become the object of historical inquiry. To be sure, Bultmann insists that the doctrinal content of the kerygma cannot be crystallized, just as the biographical details of the life of Jesus cannot be established. Yet, the fact *that (dass)* God acted in this particular event has been made the cornerstone of Bultmann's kerygmatic theology.

This stone, however, has become not only a stone of stumbling for philosophers who might wish to detour around the scandal of Christianity, it has also become the stone of stumbling for Bultmann himself. If historical criticism is valid for establishing historical facts, then it is valid for the establishment or possible disestablishment of the historicity of Jesus. The historicity of Jesus, the sheer fact that God acted, is essential to the faith of Bultmann. "But insofar as there is an essential reference to Jesus," writes Van Harvey, "it is difficult to see how faith is completely independent of historical inquiry, as Bultmann claims it is." [10] In effect, Bultmann's faith rests where he says it must not rest—on the results of historical-critical research. Bultmann, of course, cannot deny the centrality of God's action in Jesus Christ without abandoning his position as a biblical theologian. Yet, it is apparent that Bultmann's basic confession has eroded his radical criticism.

Modifications in the Elements of the Bultmannian Synthesis

Historical Criticism

At the same time that tensions have been tearing the Bultmannian synthesis asunder, the three foundations of Bultmann's structure have undergone modification. Within historical criticism a flurry of activity can be observed. The history of religions method has been employed with enthusiasm. Inspired by the discovery of the Dead Sea Scrolls, a new interest in the Jewish backgrounds of the New Testament has appeared. The same trend is visible in recent research into rabbinic sources and current efforts to find midrashic material in the New Testament. As a result, the sharp distinction between Palestinian-Jewish and Hellenistic-gentile settings has been blurred. Rather than finding the backgrounds of the Christian kerygma in Hellenism, many scholars have attempted to trace the origin of the kerygmatic elements to Jewish sources. "If one wishes to deal with the forms and contents of New Testament christology," says Riesenfeld, "it seems to be necessary to return to the elements of Jewish Messianism." [11] Robin Scroggs, a student of W. D. Davies, discerns the background of the Pauline picture of the last Adam not in the Gnostic *Urmensch* but in the "early Jewish theology of Adam." [12]

This interest in Judaism, however, has not halted the advance of Hellenistic studies. Armed with a manuscript find of their own—the discovery of the Coptic texts at Nag Hammadi—the Hellenistic scholars have charged forward under the banner of Bousset and Bultmann. Special attention has been given to the study of Gnosticism. Questions concerning the date of the sources and the definition of terms have been articulated. Is it proper to use second-century documents to discern Gnostic parallels to the New Testament? Can one speak of a pre-Christian Gnosticism, or must we characterize the syncretistic milieu of the New Testament as pre-Gnostic or proto-Gnostic? In any event, Reitzenstein's notion of a singular Gnostic redemption myth, rooted in Iranian religion and flourishing everywhere in the Graeco-Roman world, has withered under the research of scholars like Carsten Colpe and Hans-Martin Schenke. Colpe concludes that "it cannot yet be assumed that the Gnostic Redeemer doctrine is as explicit in pre-Christian times as it is claimed to be." [13] Although the debate about the existence of a pre-Christian Gnostic redemption myth continues to rage, "an impressive array of scholars," according to Edwin Yamauchi, "have come to the conclusion that the Gnostic Redeemer figure as described by Reitzenstein and Bultmann . . . is simply a post-Christian development dependent upon the figure of Christ, rather than a pre-Christian myth upon which the New Testament figure of Christ depends." [14]

What is the significance of these developments for the theological system of Rudolf Bultmann? Basically, some of his presuppositions have been put in question. The notion that the form critic can depict the differences between Jewish and Hellenistic Christianity in bold strokes and then make use of these clear outlines to trace the development of early Christian tradition has been erased. At the same time, the questionable status of the pre-Christian Gnostic redemption myth has posed questions about biblical Christology. The New Testament presentation of Christ, in Bultmann's view, followed the pattern of the descent and ascent of the Gnostic Redeemer, so that such ideas as the preexistence of Christ and the ascension of the risen Lord were judged to be pagan rather than Christian in their origin. Biblical writers like Paul simply borrowed these contemporary symbols to depict deeper theological truths. But, if the christological formulations of the New Testament should turn out to be distinctively Christian, then Bultmann's attempt to distinguish between the non-essential form (the myth) and the essential meaning (the kerygma) is frustrated. "If the pre-Christian origin and the decisive influence of the 'gnostic redeemer myth' cannot be maintained," writes Rudolf Schnackenburg, "then one of the supporting pillars of the Bultmannian edifice has collapsed." [15]

Still more varied and complex have been recent studies in the area of form criticism. For one thing, some of its most sacred presuppositions have been challenged in a most irreverent fashion. William Farmer, for example, has attacked the established two-document hypothesis and attempted to convince the scholarly world that Matthew, not Mark, is the earliest Gospel. Others, like Erhardt Güttgemanns, have charged that form criticism, once in the advance guard of the quest of the historical Jesus, has become immobile, a mere method employed in the service of trivial problems. Along with Güttgemanns, scholars of such diverse backgrounds as Eberhardt Jüngel, Humphrey Palmer, and E. P. Sanders have investigated the inadequacy of many of form criticism's methodological presuppositions. Form criticism, it has been pointed out, labored under the spell of an implicit romanticism that wrapped the origin and early form of a religious tradition in an aura of wonder. At the same time, the notion that the earliest elements of the tradition were shaped to provide illustrations for ancient Christian sermons reflected assumptions about modern preaching rather than hard evidence concerning early church history. While form critics had attempted to discover the principles of the transmission of oral tradition by researching the development of written tradition, some recent study of human communication has asserted that the transition from oral to written formulation involves a whole new understanding of language.

Contemporary Synoptic criticism has also seen a shift of focus in regard to the sources of the tradition. Whereas earlier form criticism had located much of the material in the *Sitz-im-Leben* of the church, recent research has attempted to trace the origin of more of the tradition back to the *Sitz-im-Leben* of Jesus (so Joachim Jeremias) or, in the words of Heinz Schürmann, to "the *Sitz im inneren Leben* of the pre-easter community of the disciples." [16] This means that interest was diverted from the later modification of the tradition and directed to its historical source, away from the church toward the earliest witnesses.

At the same time, a continuity was implied between the Christ of the kerygma and the historical Jesus, since the preaching of the church had its original impetus in the pre-crucifixion experience of the disciples. This refocusing of interest is likewise apparent in the latest fashion in Synoptic studies, "redaction criticism." According to this approach, attention is directed not toward the tiny units of tradition, but to the theological use which is made of traditional material in the process of editing. Rather than magnifying the role of the anonymous church, redaction criticism thrust the Gospel writers into the limelight. They were viewed not as mere editors—scissors and paste functionaries of some ancient clipping bureau—but profound theologians in their own right. Their Gospels, instead of being insignificant collections of isolated bits of tradition, were recognized to be theological documents of vast importance—documents which in their wholeness witnessed to an authentic theological confession of a creative individual. Beyond the *Sitz-im-Leben* of Jesus and the *Sitz-im-Leben* of the early community, Gospel research must recognize what Willi Marxsen has identified as "the third situation in life" [17]—the *Sitz-im-Leben* of the evangelist.

What is the meaning of these trends in form and redaction criticism for the theology of Rudolf Bultmann? For one thing, some older solutions have become problematic and a summons to restudy a host of issues has been served. The methodological presuppositions of form criticism, embraced in another theological era, require renewed scrutiny. The procedures based on those presuppositions have been refined and replaced by new historical and linguistic techniques. Besides, if the presuppositions and procedures can be called in question, then the conclusions of the form critics could be challenged as well. Humphrey Palmer, therefore, can claim that though form critics remained skeptical about the Gospel accounts, "I have shown that more 'conservative' conclusions could be reached by similar arguments." [18] More conservative conclusions would seem to be warranted, too, if it could be shown that the source of much of the tradition went back to the precrucifixion experience of the disciples—a possibility providing the means for more reliable information about the man from Nazareth, and allowing an understanding of early Christian faith as a response to the Jesus of history.

Redaction criticism, on the other hand, might appear to lend support to Bultmann's sagging position. In contrast to form criticism, whose original intent was to pursue the Jesus of history, redaction criticism focused on the theology of the Gospel writers, that is, on a relatively late stage in the development of tradition. No doubt, this change of direction diverted the scholar from the old quest, since the writers of the New Testament were preoccupied with the Christ of faith. "If the Jesus of the Gospel of Mark is the Jesus of Mark's own Christian experience and that of the church before him," writes Norman Perrin, "then the claim that the 'historical' Jesus is the center and source of Christian faith would seem to have no necessary basis in the New Testament." [19] In other words, the quest of the Jesus of history is an unbiblical endeavor. Nevertheless, the results of redaction criticism have set the Bultmannian quest of the Christ of faith in a new perspective. Rather than crediting the formulation of the faith to an anonymous community—a faceless mass, unnamed and unsophisticated—redaction criticism appraises the value of a unified confession of faith expressed by a creative theologian. It has higher appreciation of the form and content of the New Testament documents than Bultmann and the form critics were ready to express.

The more the scholar's attention was directed to the third and first life situations of the early tradition—that is, the life situations of the evangelist and of Jesus—and the more he treasured the biblical formulation of the gospel trying to trace its origin back to the pre-Christian experience of the disciples, the more he was inclined to raise questions about the second—that is, the life situation of the early community. Was the church's formulation of the tradition really so decisive? Why was it assumed that the early community's confession of faith was out of harmony with earlier and later expressions of faith? Why was it imagined that the early

Christians preached a Jesus different from the one the disciples had received? Why, finally, did Bultmann presuppose a discontinuity in regard to the Jesus of history, the Christ of the kerygma, and the Christology of the New Testament? Although a valid reason could no doubt be found in the cataclysmic experience of the resurrection (see chapter 7), there can be little question that Bultmann's liberal heritage and his dialectical reading of history have played a major role. The nineteenth-century quest of the Jesus of history assumed that historical research could serve as a weapon to destroy the false Christ of Christian dogma. Similarly, Bultmann's attempt to trace a zigzag line from Judaism's distortion of the Old Testament faith to Jesus' authentic proclamation of the Word, from Hellenism's mythological cosmology to Paul's demythologized kerygma, presupposes a pattern of discontinuity. Released from the spell of these presuppositions, more recent research is open to the possibility of greater continuity.

This possibility of continuity has lent support to the plea for resuming the quest of the historical Jesus. Actually, some scholars have continued their work almost oblivious to the notion of the Bultmannites that the old quest is dead and done for. Morton Scott Enslin, who fails to include a single title from Bultmann in his list of "useful books," invites scholars "to join those long devoted to this quest." [20] Others more aware of Bultmann's results have advocated a renewal of the quest on new ground. Joachim Jeremias, for example, acknowledges that "the dream of writing a biography of Jesus is over," [21] but believes that refinements in literary and form criticism together with new techniques in environmental and linguistic research make possible in N. A. Dahl's words "significantly surer results than the previous Life-of-Jesus literature." [22] For Jeremias, the "study of the historical Jesus . . .

is the central task of New Testament scholarship." [23] While recognizing that "faith in Christ cannot be based on historical facts," [24] these scholars believe an understanding of the history of Jesus is essential to knowing the Christ of faith. A unity exists between the historical Jesus and the Christ of the kerygma, for the one whom the Christian proclaims as Lord is none other than Jesus of Nazareth.

Some of the disciples of Bultmann, taking a different tack, have launched the "new quest of the historical Jesus." Rather than resuming the old quest, these scholars have remained loyal to Bultmann's basic understanding of history and faith. The charter of the new quest was delivered by Ernst Käsemann at a meeting of the Old Marburgers (the pupils and friends of Bultmann) in 1953. Käsemann insisted that "the life history of Jesus has its relevance for faith" [25]—a claim substantiated by the fact that the New Testament Gospels employed the tradition about the historical Jesus as a means to proclaim him Lord and Christ. The failure to take the historical Jesus seriously runs the risk of betraying the Christian message into the hands of docetism. As a matter of fact, the Jesus of history and the Christ of faith have a unity whose mutuality is essential for an adequate understanding of early Christianity. "Primitive Christianity is obviously of the opinion that the earthly Jesus cannot be understood otherwise than from the far side of Easter, that is, in his majesty as Lord of the community and that, conversely, the event of Easter cannot be adequately comprehended if it is looked at apart from the earthly Jesus." [26]

An investigation of the presuppositions and implications of this new approach has been undertaken by James M. Robinson, who coined the phrase "the new quest." Along with Gerhard Ebeling and Ernst Fuchs, Robinson sets a course according to the loadstone of existentialism. He argues that the new approach to history provides a method which can deal adequately with both Jesus and the kerygma. The kerygma, after all, is concerned with authentic self-understanding, and authentic self-understanding has come to expression in Jesus. Consequently a historical method which is essentially concerned with self-understanding is especially appropriate to interpret Jesus in a way which escapes the false objectivity of the old quest while making room for faith in the action of God in history. "If in encountering Jesus one is confronted with the same existential decision as that posed by the kerygma, one has proved all that can be proved by a new quest of the historical Jesus: not that the kerygma is true, but rather that the existential decision with regard to the kerygma is an existential decision with regard to Jesus." [27] More in accord with the themes of Käsemann, a full treatment of Jesus of Nazareth has been composed by Günther Bornkamm. He believes the message of the New Testament that God acted in the particular history of Jesus can be reduced to neither a "timeless myth" nor to "a mere saving fact," since the Gospels "bring before our eyes, in very different fashion from what is customary in chronicles and presentations of history, the historical person of Jesus with the utmost vividness." [28]

Not everyone has been swept along in the wake of the new quest. Some have suggested that the quest is not new at all, suffering the same infirmities as the old quest by making faith depend on historical research and by attempting to probe the inner life of Jesus. The most recent trend is to view the earthly Jesus as the historical person who could elicit the kind of faith confirmed by the resurrection and confessed in Christian preaching. "In short," writes Heinz Zahrnt, "Christians do not believe in a number of more or less demonstrable his-

torical facts—they believe in the person of Jesus Christ."[29]
While an exact portrait of Jesus is not possible, "we can know
important things solidly," [30] says Leander Keck; we can know
enough for Jesus to become the object of our trust. In this
sense, "the historical Jesus (the historian's Jesus) does have a
role in Christian faith." [31] Jesus is not the exclusive or absolute revelation of God in history, but, in Van Harvey's words,
a "paradigmatic event" [32]—a vivid event which illumines the
meaning of human existence. Behind the Jesus of historical
reconstruction and the biblical Christ of mythological formulation stands the actual Jesus of history whose "memory-
impression" [33] could evoke the faith of men then and now.

Thus, this most recent version of the quest stresses a continuity and unity between the Jesus of history and the Christ
of faith—a unity grounded in the actual person of history who
transcends the limitations of the modern historians and the
ancient theologians as the manifestation *of God* in history. In
this quest, the historical-critical method, for all its weaknesses
and relativity, has a positive rather than a negative significance. Bultmann's view that one cannot reconstruct the historical Jesus and that faith does not need this historical
reconstruction is superseded.

Existentialist Philosophy

Just as historical criticism has experienced changes, so too
has philosophy. Existentialism, once the oxygen of the intellectual climate, has almost dissipated. One has only to con-
sult the indexes of periodical literature to note that the stream
of essays on existentialist philosophy which once flooded the
learned journals has been reduced to a mere trickle. Already
in 1954, F. H. Heinemann could write, "The crisis and the
approaching end of Christian Existentialism are now clearly

visible." [34] The reasons for the decline and fall of the existentialist empire are complex, but there is some truth in the simple observation that existentialism is a seasonal philosophy which functions best in times of crisis, in times of war and rumors of war. This is not to say that the existential note, so often echoed in the theology of the World War II era, has been completely silenced. No one can deny that existentialism provided the theologian with an interpretative key whereby the power of the ancient texts could be unlocked and a mode of speech which could address the crucial problems of man. Yet, in spite of persistent efforts to sustain or revive existentialist theology, one is forced to conclude that philosophical endeavor, which once turned its eye inward, is now looking in other directions.

Probably a major cause for the eclipse of existentialist philosophy is its inability to project a comprehensive philosophical system. Existentialism, with its concern for concrete, individual existence, is a protest against every sort of systematizing. "This does not mean that the existentialists are unable to construct philosophies of their own," says Heinemann, "but if they do, they are bound to transcend the principle of existence." [35] Thus, the possibility that existentialism can provide a comprehensive picture of the nature of reality is ruled out in principle at the beginning. Existentialism, to be sure, does not aspire to such dizzy heights; it eschews the high peaks of metaphysics, harboring a sort of philosophical acrophobia, in order to sit at the side of the road and become a friend of man. The result, however, is a kind of reductionism in which the attempt is made to whittle the philosophical problem down to size. Consequently existentialism has difficulty in contending with ultimates and seems ready to submit to the ancient dictum that man is the measure of all things.

This inability to envisage the transcendent, this fixation on the human situation, limits existentialism's perception of the problem of God. "Due to its orientation," says Frederick Sontag, "existentialism tends to be strong on anthropology and, at best, weak on ontology and a doctrine of God." [36] The fact that existentialists come in two varieties—theistic or atheistic—indicates that the idea of God is not decisive for existentialist philosophy. In view of Bultmann's claim that "every assertion about God is simultaneously an assertion about man and vice versa," [37] "one might equally well conclude," says Schubert Ogden, "that Paul's theology may best be presented as the doctrine of God." [38] Bultmann's actual decision to present Pauline theology under the rubric of the doctrine of man makes it graphically clear that theology has been sacrificed to anthropology. This sacrifice has been purchased at too high a price in an era plagued by secularism and the announcement of the death of God. As Sontag says, "Theology's most obvious task today seems to be to develop a detailed doctrine of God, particularly one that is philosophically based." [39]

The weakness of existentialism as a basis for contemporary theological reflection is further attested by a hasty survey of the main existentialist elements in Bultmann's thought (see chapter 3). Bultmann appropriates the existentialist idea of understanding, and the resulting epistemology involves another reduction. All questions of knowledge flow through the filter of self-understanding, with the result that the larger questions about the meaning of the world and the reality of nature, so important to the contemporary scientific and technological mind, are screened out. The implied theory of knowledge is made explicit in Bultmann's assertion that demythologizing is parallel to the doctrine of justification by faith being carried "to its logical conclusion in the field of epistemology." [40]

In other words, just as man cannot get right with God on the basis of moral works, so he cannot discover truth by means of intellectual endeavor. Faith is the key to knowledge. Yet, when this faith is defined as response to the *skandalon* of the gospel which requires a risk of all old securities, a "plunge into the inner darkness," [41] one wonders if a *sacrificium intellectum*, so repugnant to Bultmann, is not being demanded. Surely we are not supposed to embrace this *skandalon* just because it is scandalous. Why should we risk our lives on this particular *skandalon* when others are ready at hand? To be sure, the faith which saves is much larger than intellectual assent to propositions, yet, as John Macquarrie points out, "the call of the existentialist for passionate participation does set in motion a tendency that . . . can indeed lead to a state of mind which conflicts with the philosopher's obligation to reason." [42] At any rate, the failure to be able to give a reason for the hope that is within is particularly embarrassing in a time when philosophy is especially preoccupied with the question of meaning and the problem of verification.

Bultmann's doctrine of man also involves a reduction. "The very nature of man," he says, "is his will." [43] This volitional anthropology, which owes much to Kant and supports Bultmann's ethic, is unduly narrow. Recent research in physiology, psychology, and anthropology provides the philosopher with sufficient raw material to construct a vastly more complex image of man. At the same time, Bultmann's concentration on the particular man in the specific situation is excessively individualistic. While this microscopic view is essential to the investigation of the basic unit of existence, it restricts one's perception of the larger dimensions of man and society. Just

as the historian cannot be removed from his participation in
history, so man cannot be extricated from his essential life
in community. One would think that a theologian who features the role of the early church in the formulation of the
gospel tradition and stresses the commandment of love of
neighbor would have a larger appreciation for the societal
aspect of man's being.

Bultmann's excessive individualism, in any case, contributes
to a similar shrinkage in the area of ethics. As Thomas Oden
says, "Bultmann is required by the narrowness of his view of
ethics to try to say all that he needs to say about decision, intention, self-knowledge, and freedom in the restricted vocabu-
lary of obedience." [44] Bultmann's existentialist understanding
of obedience, of course, allows the creation of no system of
ethics, since that would confuse man's principles with God's
nonobjective demand, turning the gospel into law. Nevertheless, Bultmann's confidence that man will know what he must
do in the particular ethical situation appears to posit an ethic
with little or no content. The content, of course, is given in the
law of love, yet, in a time of conflicting values when the mind
of man remains clouded by sin, some suggestion of what love
requires seems warranted.

Bultmann's understanding of history displays parallel
problems. History, for the existentialist, finds its meaning in
the present. The past is viewed anthropologically as a power
from which man must be freed, and the future is understood
as providing man with the present possibility of decision
about his existence. A philosophy of history which attempts to
discern some pattern in the course of history or to envisage
some goal at the end of the historical process is unthinkable.
Again, the antisystematic and nonobjective approach of existentialism has reduced history to a series of isolated points.

In Bultmann's *History and Eschatology*, the problem, according to Dorothee Soelle, "is posed by the abandonment of the question of meaning in history, that is, the reduction of the question of meaning to individual existence." [45] In Bultmann's terms, this means that the *geschichtlich* event, not the *historisch* happening, is of basic importance. Although the *geschichtlich* event occurs in the *historisch*, the former can be detected and evaluated only by the eyes of faith. Thus, the crucial aspect of history is removed from the public arena of historical and philosophical inquiry, and the uninitiated bystander is left to the mercy of anyone shouting, "Lo here! Lo there!"

When one looks beyond history to the starry heavens above, Bultmann's tunnel vision becomes even more obvious. For him, all talk about the cosmos represents an empty echo of ancient mythology. Yet, how is man able to avoid the question of the meaning of the world of nature in which he has his home—a world whose mighty forces touch his destiny. The substitution of anthropology for cosmology is an oversimplification which the philosopher can ill afford in an era when his friends are racing to the moon and shooting rockets at Mars.

In sum, Bultmann's existentialist theology, so effective in another era, does not seem to be sufficient to answer the questions the theologian faces today. In an era when man is concerned with cosmic and ecological problems, the theologian must renew his interest in the doctrine of creation. In a time when mankind seems hurtling toward destruction, the theologian should reconsider the question of the goal of history and the final destiny of mankind. In a period when man is isolated in loneliness, when the dearth of meaningful community is everywhere apparent, when traditional institutions stand under heavy attack, the theologian must turn his attention anew

to the doctrine of the church. In a time when man is facing
large and ambiguous ethical decisions, when he is urged, on
the one hand, to reduce his morality to an easy relativity, or,
on the other, to surrender his freedom to some ancient legalism, the theologian must search for an ethic which has content without law—an ethic which can cope not only with the
lonely decisions of the solitary man of faith but also with the
larger social and political questions which challenge the
viability of the people of God.

Dialectical Theology

The devaluation of existentialism was accompanied by the
debasing of dialectical theology. More than a decade ago
William Hordern observed that the time was "post-neo-
orthodox," [46] and Langdon Gilkey has written of the "demise
of neo-orthodoxy." [47] The brand of theology which was mar-
keted in most divinity schools and which was consumed in the
ecumenical dialogue twenty-five years ago has virtually dis-
appeared. A major cause of neoorthodoxy's decline has been
suspicion about the basic dialectic. The dialectical theologians, enchanted by Kierkegaard's idea of the infinite qualitative distinction between time and eternity, perceived a vision
of reality in which God was distant from the world. But why
must it be assumed, especially by theologians who abhor
metaphysics, that reality bears this dialectical structure? To
be sure, the error of confusing the creation with the Creator
is at least as old as Paul, but, more important, the religion
which the dialectical theologians opposed was marked by that
same confusion. The faith of the nineteenth century was a
culture-religion involving a union between the values of
society and vestiges of the Christian tradition. Jesus was
portrayed in Victorian garb—the heroic realization of man's

noblest aspirations. While dialectical theology was justified in putting the ax to this distorted picture, it may have shattered elements important for the Christian faith. Was transcendence purchased at the price of immanence? Was God promoted out of reach? In any case, the result has been called in Hermann Timm's terms an "acosmic kerygmatic theology" —a theology characterized by "de-worldlification." [48]

By way of contrast, a current trend in theology is ready to affirm the participation of God in the life of the world. This affirmation recognizes that the God whose ways are not our ways is also the Lord who is "near to all who call upon him" (Ps. 145:18). With such a God it is possible for man to have communion, and communion between God and man would appear to be a fundamental precept of the Christian doctrine of revelation. The confession that the Word became flesh implies that man is the kind of being who can embody the eternal Word, and that the Word is the sort of divine reality which can come in human form. Consequently, contemporary biblical theology is concerned, according to Hans-Joachim Kraus, with "neither an isolated man nor an isolated God, but God and man in their meeting and community which was founded and accomplished by God himself in the act (or acts) of revelation." [49] This positive relationship between God and man is even more highly valued in process theology. There, where God is defined as the creative process at work in the world, the gap between God and man is bridged. God's being, or becoming, includes finitude and temporality, and man's being participates in the divine process. As John Cobb says, "We are literally in God and God is literally in us." [50]

From a totally different perspective, Ulrich Mauser has recently argued that anthropomorphism is a basic and valid feature of biblical theology. In the imagery of the Bible, God is often depicted in the form of man and man in the form of God. While this imagery sometimes reflects primitive theological conceptions, much of the ancient symbolism points to a deeper truth: that God participates with man in human history. Although already perceived by the prophets, the idea that God is affected by his participation in history and that man is able to participate in the suffering of God reaches its supreme expression in Jesus Christ. "The New Testament is thus the fulfillment of the Old Testament, since in the human life of Jesus Christ the anthropomorphism of God and the theomorphism of man have been accomplished in history." [51]

In sharp distinction from Mauser, some contemporary theologians are questioning dialectical theology's preoccupation with the revelation of God in Christ. Perceptive critics schooled in analytic philosophy believe the whole concept of revelation to be problematic. While Christians talk about a revelation which has occurred, their unwillingness to attribute content to this revelation suggests that nothing has been revealed. A revelation which is subject to neither verification nor falsification represents a failure to consider the question of religious meaning "by default through ambiguities and confusions in crucial terms." [52] Theologians of more orthodox persuasion, while acknowledging the validity of God's revelation in Christ, charge dialectical theology with magnifying the Christ-event out of proper proportion. H. Richard Niebuhr, for example, protests against "the tendency in much post-liberal theology . . . to base on a few passages of the New Testament a new unitarianism of the second person of the Trinity." [53] Similarly, G. Ernest Wright asserts that "the Christian Old Testament scholar . . . must reject certain varieties of Christocentricity which dissolve theology into Christology." [54] To be sure, if getting right with God depends exclusively on the particular event of Jesus of Nazareth, then one can only feel sorry for Abraham, Moses, and the prophets, let alone the aborigines of the South Sea Islands. To stress the particularity of God's self-disclosure in Jesus, of course, belongs to the valid conviction that revelation must come to man in his concrete situation with all its humanness and historicity. Yet, to make this historically conditioned revelation into an absolute seems to limit God's activity and to force God's revelation into man's mold. Paul, for all his devotion to the particularity and foolishness of the cross, still insists that Abraham, who never saw Jesus, was saved by faith—faith in the God who in the end will be all in all. The claim to the fullness of God's revelation in Christ belongs to the essence of Christianity, but that claim must be made with a humility which is consistent with the Jesus who said, "Why do you call me good?" (Mark 10:18).

Basic to Bultmann's idea of revelation is his understanding of eschatology. God reveals himself by an act occurring in history and recurring in the word of proclamation—an eschatological act. It is therefore striking that this cornerstone of Bultmannian theology has been undermined by a theologian of the Bultmann school, Ernest Käsemann. In contrast to Bultmann's existentialist eschatology which "reduces God's future to men's futurity," [55] Käsemann detects in the New Testament an understanding of history forged in the fires of Jewish apocalypticism. Jesus was himself an apocalyptic teacher, and the early Christians expected him soon to appear as an apocalyptic figure, the majestic Son of Man. This attention to the future indicates that the earliest formulators of Christian tradition had an interest in the course and outcome of history. Käsemann is thus led to the startling conclusion that apocalyptic, once despised as the illegitimate offspring of

Jewish infidelity, is in truth "the mother of all Christian theology." [56] If Käsemann should prove to be correct, Bultmann's eschatological thread running from Jesus to Paul and finally to John will turn out to be synthetic, spun in Marburg with scarcely a fiber from the New Testament.

While not everyone has hailed Käsemann's conclusion, his effort to hoist the banner of apocalypticism has enlisted support for new attempts to revive salvation-history theology. Wolfhart Pannenberg, a leader of the revival, believes that God's revelation in history is always indirect. Only at the end of history, only when God has fulfilled his purpose for man and the world, will God's self-disclosure be complete. Yet, though the end is beyond the vision of the believer, an event has occurred in history which unveils that future—the resurrection of Jesus, a "proleptic event" which reveals what the end is all about. "Only because the end of the world is already present in Jesus' resurrection," says Pannenberg, "is God himself revealed in him." [57] Thus, an apocalyptic event in history discloses history's ultimate apocalyptic outcome. Far from being a discarded remnant of Jewish mythology, apocalypticism is the proper garb of the Christian theologian. The resurrection of Jesus—the apocalyptic event basic to Pannenberg's view of history—can be established by hard-headed historical argument, so that faith, rather than being a leap into the void, is built on the solid rock of historical fact.

Pannenberg's concern for the future is pursued further by Jürgen Moltmann, the originator of the theology of hope. Indeed, the trouble with Pannenberg, in Moltmann's opinion, is his restricted understanding of the future—a future predetermined by a past event. According to Moltmann, the God of the future is the God of surprises, as the resurrection of Jesus suggests. History, therefore, must be viewed as "open to

God and to the future." [58] That the future will unfold God's final triumph so that it can be anticipated with joy is already illuminated by the glory of the risen Christ. But what secrets the future will unveil, what God will do to bring it in, these things man cannot ascertain. As Paul says, "Who hopes for what he sees?" (Rom. 8:24).

Having shot down Bultmann's eschatology with a blast from Jewish apocalyptic, Ernst Käsemann has proceeded to take aim at his teacher's idea of justification by faith. As we have seen (chapter 5), Bultmann understands his program of demythologizing to be parallel to the Reformation principle of justification. He conceives of righteousness as an event, as the decisive eschatological act of God which encounters the solitary individual and calls him to radical obedience and authentic self-understanding. Käsemann argues, however, that Paul's phrase "the righteousness of God" does not mean the righteousness from God—an act of which God is the author— but rather that it describes *God's own* righteousness. The theme of the Epistle to the Romans is not God's action which announces or imputes righteousness to man—an event in history and in preaching—but instead, the vindication of God's rightness.

Käsemann concludes, "All that we have been saying amounts to this: *righteousness of God* is for Paul God's sovereignty over the world revealing itself eschatologically in Jesus." [59] Since righteousness includes sovereignty over the world, the righteousness of God has a cosmic dimension, and this point is sharpened by Käsemann's student, Peter Stuhlmacher. Another pupil, Christian Müller, has argued, against Bultmann's individualism, that the righteousness of God means belonging to the people of God. According to the Käsemann position, Bultmann's perception of the righteousness of

God is too narrow, missing the wider vistas of creation and history.

For Bultmann, the deed of God's righteousness occurs in the word of preaching. His theology is a kerygmatic theology, and the unity of the New Testament, insofar as it exists at all, is found in the concept of the word. Yet, just this central element of Bultmann's theology has come under scrutiny in recent research. James Barr, for instance, believes the attempt to characterize the biblical understanding of the word as dynamic event, in contrast with a more noetic Greek idea, presupposes a false distinction between Hebrew and Hellenic modes of thought and expression.

On the other hand, another contemporary theologian attacks "the tendency which is latent in every theology of the Word to wed religious experience to matters of the intellect." [60] This latter charge would seem to fit some of Bultmann's followers better than the master himself. For example, the devotees of the new hermeneutic, taking their cue from the more recent works of Heidegger, have assigned to language a major role in the search for reality. According to Heidegger, language is the house of being, that is, language is the fundamental element in existence. This means that the new hermeneutic, in contrast to the old, is not a collection of rules for the interpretation of an ancient text, but a whole new way of thinking. As James M. Robinson says, "The new hermeneutic is a new theology. . . . theology itself is hermeneutic." [61]

According to this new theology, speaking the word brings reality into expression and is viewed as an event of disclosure, a speech-event (Ernst Fuchs) or word-event (Gerhard Ebeling). The decisive speech-event is Jesus Christ, for, as Fuchs says, "Jesus claimed to bring God himself decisively 'into language.' " [62] For Bultmann, the exegete interprets the text to discern its meaning for his self-understanding; the text remains the object. Following the implications of Bultmann's approach to its logical conclusion, the practitioners of the new hermeneutic give self-understanding its proper place; the interpreter is the object of interpretation. We do not interpret the text; the text interprets us.

Taking account of all these recent theological trends, the main reason for the decline of dialectical theology is the changing climate of contemporary culture. Man, in tune with the times, no longer sings,

> I am a stranger here,
> within a foreign land.

He has forsaken Mount Pisgah's lofty heights to migrate east of Eden to the cities of the plain. In the secular city, the "strange new world of the Bible" seemed all too strange to have modern meaning. To the younger initiates of the theological cult, the God who had broken into history seemed remote. They had seen no mighty acts, heard no dynamic word. In this atmosphere, polluted by secularity, the biblical theology movement which had reached such vigor under the inspiration of Bultmann breathed its last. The eulogy was delivered by Bishop Robinson, who while being *Honest to God* was not true to the Bible. Although the new hermeneuts with their fancy linguistics were talking about "translating what the Bible has to say into the word for today," [63] many people today do not care what the Bible has to say at all. Surely the theology of the Word represents a last-ditch attempt to defend the faith delivered all too long ago unto the saints. As Langdon Gilkey says, "No longer can the theologian or biblical scholar merely appeal to the 'biblical view' as an assumed theological authority, since the questions of whether there be a revelation or a revealer at all are the ones he must deal with." [64]

In this chapter, no calculated effort has been made to evaluate the arguments and research surveyed. That tensions exist within the Bultmannian structure and that the foundations of the structure have undergone modification—these points seem apparent. Some of the arguments advanced against Bultmann's position bear more weight than others, and some of the research summarized has greater significance than the rest. Strong defenses against the anti-Bultmann attacks are easy to muster, for example, Eduard Lohse's answer to Käsemann's fascination with apocalypticism, and Günter Klein's response to the new understanding of the righteousness of God. What has been included here is a selection of recent research and argument which indicates that the Bultmannian synthesis cannot endure, that we are now in the post-Bultmann era.

Of course, to charge that a synthesis of historical criticism, existentialist philosophy, and dialectical theology is inadequate for today casts no blanket of condemnation over the magnificent accomplishment of Rudolf Bultmann. A theology can never be justly evaluated in the time of its decline, but at the moment of its zenith, in terms of its power to speak prophetically to the demands of that day. The era of Nazi Germany was a time for burning, not for reason. Members of the ecclesiastical resistance, many of them disciples of Bultmann, as they were cast into concentration camps and herded into Russian prisons, had no time for cosmological speculation or programs of social action—theirs was a time for decision, of man alone in the crisis of faith.

Chapter 7

Christo Who Goes Before You

A New Quest of the Christ of Faith

ALTHOUGH WE MAY GAZE wistfully at the era of Bultmann, we
must bid it farewell. No theologian knows better than Rudolf
Bultmann that he who looks back turns into a pillar of salt.
However, as we look ahead, what have we learned from the
past? What has the era of biblical theology furnished us for
the facing of these days? Can a biblical theology survive in a
secular society? Has man-come-of-age outgrown not only
Bible stories but the story of the Bible? And what of the quest
for the Christ of faith? Has it bogged down in the rubble of
Bultmann's crumbling system, mired in the shifting sands of
biblical and theological research? Should modern man with
his sights set on the future look back for guidance to a figure
of the past, or has the Christ of faith burst the bonds of time
and space to go before us into Galilee?

In Search of a Theological Synthesis

At the outset, we may observe that a vigorous biblical theology will require some sort of theological synthesis. Just as the theology of Bultmann flourished in a climate of theological renaissance, so a revival of biblical thought will take root in a soil enriched by the essential theological elements. Among these will be a basic and comprehensive *ontology*—a theory of being which purports to make sense out of the whole. This total world view must include in its perspective not only a vision of the meaning of history, but also a panoramic perception of the whole vista of cosmic reality. This ontology, particularly in our time of pervasive secularity, must be prepared to grapple with the problem of the transcendent, to deal clearly and profoundly with the problem of God.

At the same time, a theological synthesis which intends to remain Christian will have to include in its comprehensive view of reality a high valuation of the *Christian tradition*—the faith once for all delivered to the saints and passed down in a variety of forms to a succession of sinners. This legacy from the past will treasure the concepts of God's revelation in history, the Word made flesh, the witness of the Scriptures, the faithfulness of the people of God. These treasures are valued because Christianity is a historical religion, that is, a religion whose basic components are provided by history. The Christian faith is not primarily preoccupied with abstract principles; it focuses its concern on events and their meaning. This is why biblical theology, without attempting to dominate the stage, must continue to play an important role in the theological drama. Biblical theology is no super kind of systematics, but only a division of historical theology which directs its attention to a particular segment of history—

the history of God's revelatory and redemptive deeds. Of course, this high valuation of revelation, the Bible, and tradition cannot demand the mortgage of man's intellect; it must be assessed in terms of the comprehensive vision of reality and commend itself to the rational structure of man's whole being.

Since a valid theological synthesis will have to reckon with historical revelation, it will need to employ a *method* which can adequately investigate the course and meaning of history. The historical-critical method, for all its effectiveness in the past, needs further refinements and a new sensitivity to human problems—a sensitivity not always perceptible to techniques developed in the scientific laboratory. Moreover, the method used to investigate and interpret history must be consistent with the theological method used elsewhere within the theological synthesis—the method, for example, used in the explication of the doctrine of God.

The theological-historical method should be grounded in the fundamental ontology, which means that attention must be given to the problems of methodology and the question of the nature and meaning of history. At the same time, the new theological synthesis will need to wrestle with the hermeneutical question, that is, the question of how a comprehensive ontology or a theological tradition can be translated into meaning for modern man. While it is mistaken to suppose that modern man is the piper who calls the theological tune, a valid and vital theology must always speak forcefully to the crucial problems of man in his contemporary setting. As Paul would say, How can man believe unless he has heard?

Who is sufficient for these things? The harvest is vast and the laborers few, awed by the achievement of their predecessors, ill-equipped for the needs of the day. Ours is not a

time of theological synthesis. Yesterday's theological garden
of Eden has turned into a wasteland, and theologians once
feeding on the tree of knowledge find themselves laboring by
the sweat of their brows. The followers of Barth and Bultmann appear to be replowing old ground hardly aware of the
fact that they have been driven out of paradise. The new
theologies have scarcely taken root, let alone grown into
sturdy plants. Few things seem so dead as the death of God
theology, and Harvey Cox's secular city has become a theological ghost town, populated by a host of specters seeking some
ray of transcendence amid the shadows of mysterious cults.
The theology of the future, recently flashing across the heavens
in the brilliant constellation of Pannenberg and Moltmann,
seems already to have faded and become a thing of the past.

In this time of confusion, the biblical theologian may have
to jettison his hope for synthesis and sail into the troubled
waters of pluralism, seeking a harbor for his anthropology
here, and his Christology there. Yet, to those schooled in the
Judaeo-Christian tradition of monotheism, this seems to be a
tentative solution at best—a sort of temporary submission to
the many gods as they await the Word of the one Lord. In contrast to an easy pluralism, more hopeful is the work of two
groups of American theologians who are projecting theological structures from the perspectives of metaphysics or history. On the one hand, students of Charles Hartshorne have
found in Whiteheadian process philosophy the ontological
ground for a theology which can grapple with the cosmic problem while continuing, especially in the work of Schubert Ogden and John Cobb, to take seriously the Christian tradition
and even discuss the finality of Christ. On the other hand,
students of H. Richard Niebuhr, particularly Van Harvey and
Gordon Kaufman, who acknowledge the importance of historical revelation and employ a methodology which can speak

meaningfully about the acts of God, are attempting to comprehend the whole of reality from a historicist's perspective. What may be the outcome of these ambitious efforts only time will tell. In any event, the historian of theology knows well that theological syntheses are born not made, that they come only in the fullness of time.

In Quest of the Christ of Faith

Although a viable theological synthesis may not be currently in view, the student of the Bible cannot shirk his basic tasks, despite his theological limitations. He will continue to assume, even lacking an adequate theological structure, that the message of the Bible, because of the primacy of its witness to historical revelation, is significant. But, if the ground of the Bultmannian quest of the Christ of faith has proved shaky, is it possible to launch a new quest? Is a new quest of the Christ of faith possible and theologically legitimate?

At the outset, it will be appropriate to clarify the basic terms. Five fundamental concepts are crucial to the following discussion.

1. The *Jesus of history*, that is, Jesus of Nazareth, the man who lived in Galilee two thousand years ago.

2. The *historical Jesus*, that is, the historical reconstruction of the words and deeds of Jesus accomplished by critical research.

3. The *Christ of the kerygma*, that is, the Christ who was proclaimed by the early church as Messiah and living Lord.

4. The *kerygmatic Christ*, that is, the Christ of Christian doctrine constructed by theological analysis and reflection.

5. The *Christ of faith*, that is, the Christ who is somehow

present to man today, the Christ in whom modern man can put his trust.

The possibility of the quest of the Christ of faith appears to be acknowledged on every hand. Diverse religious expressions all the way from the popular Jesus movement, with its naïve biblicism and its aberrant Christology, to the sophisticated historical quests, with their concern for hermeneutic and historical method, represent various efforts to make Jesus accessible for faith. In other words, the quest of the Christ of faith has been proved to be possible by the sheer fact that hosts of people yesterday and today have been able to make Jesus Christ the focal point around which their lives can be meaningfully oriented. The Christ of faith, as a matter of fact, is the central concern of most of these movements—even the quest of the historical Jesus. That quest has usually been moved by theological interest and seldom by mere antiquarian concerns.

At its beginning, the old quest was designed to destroy the dogmatic Christ and establish a valid ground for faith in Jesus. The new quest, in its varying forms, is anxious to show how Jesus is a model for faith or the personal object of man's trust. As the old quest, the new quests are engaged in a theological task—a task whereby Jesus is made meaningful for modern man's faith. Theologians engaged in this task are not content to restore Jesus accurately as a museum's monument to the past, even if that were possible for a historian who participates in the history he interprets. The quest of the historical Jesus is an attempt to bring Jesus into the present experience of the historian, to discern his significance for theological reconstruction. In short, it is an aspect of the quest of the Christ of faith.

In considering the question of the possibility of this quest, it is important to ask: Can Jesus Christ be understood as an object worthy of trust? The attempt to answer this question demands that we weigh anchor and sail into a theological maelstrom—the problem of revelation. If God is really God —the transcendent being, Maker of heaven and earth, Lord of history—then he cannot be known as some ordinary object. God is too big for man to wrap his mind around. He can only be known as he participates in man's experience so as to disclose himself.

Moreover, if God is to disclose himself in a manner which is meaningful for man and still consistent with his own transcendence, then he must reveal himself at the highest level of human perception. That is the level of man's transcendent personality, for man in his essential personal being cannot be known, just as God cannot be known, as an object. One cannot come to know a person by memorizing his vital statistics, but only by entering into a personal relationship, a relationship of self-disclosure in mutual commitment.

If the highest level of man's perception is the level of personal reality, we may argue analogically that God's revelation must be a personal revelation. According to the Christian confession, that revelation has occurred in history in the person of Jesus Christ. To be sure, one cannot first prove that Christ is God's revelation and then decide to entrust one's life to him, just as one does not check a person's credit rating before accepting him as a friend. First one must trust, and then in the mutuality and continuing experience of trust learn what friendship means. This is what the New Testament calls faith —personal trust in God's personal revelation in Jesus Christ. That the mutuality of this personal experience cannot be reduced to a moment of encounter, an empty *Dass*, a point in history, ought to be abundantly clear. Of course, the sign that

faith is possible and appropriate is already given in the quality and character of the object of faith. That Jesus is really
trustworthy, that he is fully personal, that he comes with the
gift of love, that he commits himself to man—all this is evident to those who open their eyes.

Yet, how is it possible, even with open eyes, to view a figure
of the distant past? What kind of a telescopic sight is available to make possible for modern man the quest of the Christ
of faith? As anyone who reads history knows, persons of the
past can be appropriated by the mind of man and become the
source of insight into reality, the basis for an understanding
of humanity, the spark of inspiration for action. In the same
way, Jesus can become the object of faith for the modern
Christian. The Scriptures which record his words and deeds
also include the response which men made to him; they represent the fullness of revelation as involving both God's self-
disclosure and man's personal commitment. Alongside the
Bible and dependent on the history it records, a living line of
memory extends from the present back through the community
of faith to the earliest witnesses of Jesus as the Christ.
Throughout this line of continually renewed personal experience, the vitality of the original revelatory experience is preserved in a way which is both faithful to the historical
revelation and vital for contemporary faith.

In everyday experience, we sometimes have the assurance
that we know a person we have never met simply on the basis
of what someone else has witnessed about him, so that when we
finally meet, we say, "I feel I've known you all along!" Oc-
casionally the added remark is made, "You don't look like I
expected; I thought you would be tall and thin!" Yet, after the
mutuality which has already been established is acknowledged, and the relationship is continued and deepened, then

the conviction, "I knew you all along," is confirmed. Some people count among their closest friends persons whom they have seen only a few times, but the living witness of mutual friends makes the distant relationship a vital reality. In the same way, the historical record and response carried on in the living tradition of the community and present in the witness of faith make the quest of the Christ of faith a present possibility.

Yet, if the quest of the Christ of faith is possible, is the quest also theologically legitimate? The answer, of course, depends on what kind of a Christ one is called to have faith in. If the revelation of God occurred in history, then it is evident that a proper understanding of the Christ of faith will have some relation to the Jesus of history. In the light of our definitions, however, it is clear that Jesus in some ways cannot become faith's legitimate object. The *historical Jesus*—the Jesus constructed by historical criticism—cannot be a proper object of faith, since that object would be a fallible human construction. Moreover, to insist that modern historical reconstruction is essential to faith would imply that Christians before the Enlightenment, before the discovery of the historical-critical method, had no faith at all—a conclusion denied by a cursory reading of the history of the church.

No, the object of faith is not the historical Jesus, but the *Jesus of history*—the person in whom God acted to reveal his character and purpose, the person who represents the transcendence of God. But what, then, is the role of historical research in the quest of the Christ of faith? Although the historical critical method needs refinement and increased sensitivity, it remains the best method available to discover what Jesus said and did in order to perceive what God revealed through him. The belief that Christ emptied himself to take on historical form means that he is subjected to historical existence and the scrutiny of the historians. As a matter of fact, throughout the history of the church faith has been involved in historical research, for the whole Christian tradition is a witness to what happened in history. The New Testament documents represent the work of "historians" who, like Luke, "followed all things closely . . . to write an orderly account" (Luke 1:3), or, like the writer of 1 John testified to that "which we have heard, which we have seen with our eyes, which we have looked upon and touched with our hands" (1 John 1:1).

Does this imply that the modern historian with his more sophisticated tools can turn out a better model for faith? Not at all! For one thing, it is not certain that the modern method is that much better; it may be an impediment to historical understanding, a hang-up of our limited scientific world view. But, more important, the Jesus of history (in contrast to the historical Jesus) is not identical with any objective reconstruction. As we have seen, a person cannot be known the way we come to comprehend some objective entity. Just as a student is not identical with his letters of recommendation or even the picture on his application, so Jesus is not to be identified with any historical records or reconstruction of him no matter how accurate they may be. To be sure, our knowledge of the Jesus of history is communicated through records and reconstruction, just as our knowledge of a person is communicated through physical data which he gives or which is given about him. Yet, just as the person is not to be equated with the media through which he is made known, so Jesus transcends all the records and reconstructions. What the earliest "historians" recorded were signs pointing to the person of God's revelation; that Jesus was born of woman, that he proclaimed the rule of God, that he declared the law of love, that he died on the cross, that he appeared to his followers—all this was formed into a fine lens, transparent in itself, but bringing into focus the object of faith.

If the historical Jesus is not a proper object of faith, neither is the *kerygmatic Christ*—the Christ of theological reconstruction. Sometimes it is supposed that faith in Christ means intellectual assent to christological doctrines, for example, the statements about the nature and work of Christ found in the New Testament or early Christian creeds. This view is blind to the fact that these christological formulations were shaped in another time using signs and symbols of a distant culture. Terms like *logos* and *kurios* have their meaning in a context which is beyond our contemporary vision. As we have learned from the advocates of the "new hermeneutic," the translation of the same concept into a different setting demands a change of language. Moreover, the notion that faith is assent to christological doctrine assumes a false view of faith. Faith is not essentially belief that doctrines are true—"even the demons believe" (James 2:19)—but personal commitment to God's revelation in Christ. One cannot entrust his life to a doctrine, but only to a person. This is the meaning of the ancient slogan, "No creed but Christ"—that the object of faith is not a set of doctrines but a personal reality who transcends all creedal formulation.

If neither the historical Jesus nor the kerygmatic Christ is appropriate, what is the proper understanding of Christ as object of faith? Or, to put the question another way, How can the Jesus of history become the *Christ of faith*? The answer to this question involves the complicated problem of continuity. What needs to be demonstrated is that there is a line of connection from the Jesus of history through the Christ of the kerygma to the Christ of faith, in other words, that God's revelation in Jesus which was the object of early Christian witness can become the object of man's faith today.

At the outset, it is important to recognize that a degree of discontinuity is involved in the transition from the Jesus of history to the Christ of the kerygma. Easter was the dawning of a new day; the Jesus of the cross had been transformed into the spiritual body and the disciples who had fled in fear returned to Jerusalem to declare him Lord and Christ. Yet, in most cases, those who witnessed the resurrection appearances had been prepared to open their eyes by some previous relation with Jesus. The conviction that God had acted in the raising of Christ rested in no small measure upon what the disciples had already perceived God to be doing in the life of Jesus—that the power of God was at work in him, that the rule of God was anticipated in him, that Jesus was the sort of man God would designate as Lord and Christ. Indeed, faith in the Christ of the kerygma—the Christ proclaimed as risen Lord —had its source in the Jesus of history—the person who lived in Galilee and challenged the disciples to follow him.

This continuity between the Jesus of history and the Christ of the kerygma suggests that the Jesus of history is a criterion for Christian preaching. It was for this reason that the early church relatively late in its life continued to write Gospels. At a time when the very existence of the church was threatened by a spiritual enthusiasm which supposed that direct revelation was available, when it was imagined that the Spirit had shortcircuited God's revelation in history, when a docetic Gnosticism denied that Christ had come in the flesh, it was essential to declare that God had revealed himself decisively in Jesus of Nazareth.

Although a precise historical reconstruction is not possible, the Jesus who stands behind the historical record and the early Christian witness can in his basic life and character be perceived, and this Jesus stands in judgment on the false Christs of man's imagination. All sorts of bizarre activities—everything from beating one's wife to splitting the church—have been promoted in the name of Christ. Against this kind of Gnosticism, the Jesus of history exclaims, "Satan, get thee hence!" Each strange murmuring of the spirit must be exposed to the clear Christian confession, "Jesus is Lord." Not all the murmurings, of course, will evoke an easy yes or no, but the Jesus of history will provide a fundamental criterion for discerning which spirits are from God. For all the problems created by the stumbling block of Christian particularity, the conviction that God's revelation is essentially historical and personal requires that revelation occur in a particular person at a particular time.

The problem of particularity, however, does complicate the question of continuity. Although a continuity exists between the Jesus of history and the Christ of the kerygma, how is it possible for the Jesus of history to become the contemporary Christ without losing his particularity? The answer is that the revelation in Jesus is the revelation *of God*. God transcends the medium of his revelation. In order to reveal God to man, the revealer must empty himself, become poor, be obedient to death, and, in the end, deliver the kingdom to the Father. Jesus was fully conscious of this truth, always pointing away from himself to God. To the query, "Good teacher," Jesus replied, "Why do you call me good? No one is good but God alone" (Mark 10:18). In accepting the crucifixion—the most certain historical event of his career and the key to understanding his life—Jesus reveals his intent to be absolutely obedient to the will and purpose of God.

This conduct of Jesus is instructive for our own under-

standing of the particularity of God's revelation. Although
the Christian must acknowledge the claim of the fullness of
the revelation of God in Jesus Christ, he can never make that
claim in pride. To suppose that the Christian can run about
touting the superiority of his faith is totally inconsistent with
the criterion of the radical humility of Jesus, a denial of the
foolishness of the cross. What the Christian affirms, however,
is that at one particular point in history he perceives the
revelation of what God has been doing all along.

The revelation in Jesus Christ is not some new tactic lately
introduced into God's strategy of redemption, but the wisdom
of God, decreed before the ages. What we have seen and
heard in Jesus is what God has ever been and even now is
doing—taking part in human suffering and calling his people
to deeds of love.

Beyond the historical Jesus, beyond the kerygmatic Christ,
stands the eternal Christ—the revelatory and redemptive
being of God—who became incarnate in the Jesus of history
and was proclaimed the Christ of the kerygma. In this living
Christ it is possible for man to have faith, since he is the
wisdom and power of God—Jesus Christ, "the same yesterday and today and forever" (Heb. 13:8).

Notes

Chapter 1

1. Günther Bornkamm, *Jesus of Nazareth,* p. 13. Full information on this book, and most of the others referred to in the notes, is given in the bibliography. Books not listed in the bibliography are cited in full in the notes.

2. Albert Schweitzer, *The Quest of the Historical Jesus,* p. 398.

3. Ibid., p. 399.

4. James M. Robinson, *A New Quest of the Historical Jesus,* pp. 26 ff.

5. Martin Kähler, *The So-Called Historical Jesus and the Historic Biblical Christ,* p. 72.

6. Bernhard W. Anderson, "The Crisis in Biblical Theology," *Theology Today* 28 (1971):322.

7. Cf., Krister Stendahl, "Method in the Study of Biblical Theology," in J. Philip Hyatt, ed., *The Bible in Modern Scholarship* (New York: Abingdon Press, 1965), pp. 196 ff.

8. Cf., Brevard S. Childs, *Biblical Theology in Crisis* (Philadelphia: Westminster Press, 1970).

Chapter 2

1. Adolf Harnack, *What Is Christianity?*, p. 6.
2. Wilhelm Bousset, *Kyrios Christos*, p. 267.
3. Wilhelm Bousset, *The Faith of a Modern Protestant*, trans. F. B. Low (New York: Charles Scribner's Sons, 1909), p. 118.
4. Rudolf Bultmann, "Introduction," in Harnack, *What Is Christianity*, p. x.
5. Rudolf Bultmann, *Primitive Christianity*, p. 79.
6. Rudolf Bultmann, "The Concept of the Word of God in the New Testament," in Robert W. Funk, ed., *Faith and Understanding*.:306.
7. Shirley Jackson Case, *The Evolution of Early Christianity*, p. 364.
8. Shirley Jackson Case, *The Social Origins of Christianity*, p. 23.
9. Carl Kraeling, *Anthropos and Son of Man*, p. 190.
10. Martin Dibelius, *From Tradition to Gospel*, p. 295.
11. Burton Scott Easton, *The Gospel before the Gospels*, p. 49.
12. Rudolf Bultmann, "The New Approach to the Synoptic Problem," in *Existence and Faith*, p. 36.
13. Ibid., p. 51.
14. Ibid., p. 44.
15. Vincent Taylor, *The Formation of the Gospel Tradition*, p. 41.
16. Erich Fascher, *Die formgeschichtliche Methode*, p. 223.
17. Easton, *Gospel before the Gospels*, p. 60.
18. Ibid., p. 77.
19. Glenn W. Barker, William L. Lane, J. Ramsey Michaels, *The New Testament Speaks* (New York: Harper & Row, 1969), p. 69.
20. R. H. Lightfoot, *History and Interpretation in the Gospels*, p. 225.
21. Rudolf Bultmann and Karl Kundsin, *Form Criticism: Two Essays on New Testament Research*, trans. F. C. Grant (New York: Harper & Row, Harper Torchbooks, 1962), p. 8.
22. Rudolf Bultmann, *Jesus and the Word*, p. 8.
23. Rudolf Bultmann, "New Testament and Mythology," in Hans Werner Bartsch, ed., *Kerygma and Myth: A Theological Debate*, trans. R. H. Fuller, vol. 1 (New York: Harper & Bros., 1961), p. 15.
24. Bultmann, *Jesus and the Word*, p. 217.

Chapter 3

1. John E. Smith, "Existential Philosophy," in Marvin Halverson and Arthur A. Cohen, eds., *Handbook of Christian Theology* (New York: Meridian Books, 1958), p. 120.

2. Martin Heidegger, "What Is Metaphysics," in Werner Brock, ed., *Existence and Being* (Chicago: Henry Regnery, 1949), p. 325.

3. Rudolf Bultmann, "Autobiographical Reflections," in *Existence and Faith*, p. 288.

4. Rudolf Bultmann, "The Concept of Revelation in the New Testament," in *Existence and Faith*, p. 64.

5. Rudolf Bultmann, "The Understanding of Man and the World in the New Testament and in the Greek World," in *Essays—Philosophical and Theological*, p. 72.

6. Rudolf Bultmann, *History and Eschatology*, p. 94.

7. Rudolf Bultmann, *Theology of the New Testament*, 1:191.

8. Rudolf Bultmann, "The Question of 'Dialectic' Theology," in James M. Robinson, ed., *The Beginnings of Dialectic Theology*, trans. K. R. Crim and L. DeGrazia (Richmond: John Knox Press, 1968), 1:267.

9. Rudolf Bultmann, "What Does It Mean to Speak of God?" in Funk, ed., *Faith and Understanding*, 1:61.

10. Rudolf Bultmann, *Jesus Christ and Mythology*, p. 72.

11. Schubert Ogden, in Bultmann, *Existence and Faith*, p. 14.

12. Bultmann, *Theology of the New Testament*, 1:194.

13. Ibid., 227.

14. Ibid., 238.

15. Ibid., 245.

16. Ibid., 246.

17. Ibid., 259.

18. Bultmann, "New Testament and Mythology," 1:30.

19. Bultmann, *History and Eschatology*, pp. 18 f.

20. Rudolf Bultmann, "History and Eschatology in the New Testament," *New Testament Studies* 1 (1954–55):13.

21. Bultmann, "New Testament and Mythology," 1:36.

22. Rudolf Bultmann, *Jesus and the Word*, p. 21.

23. Bultmann, *Jesus Christ and Mythology*, p. 32.

24. Bultmann, "History and Eschatology in the New Testament," p. 14.

25. Ibid., p. 13.

26. Rudolf Bultmann, "Jesus and Paul," in *Existence and Faith*, p. 200.

27. Rudolf Bultmann, "The Problem of a Theological Exegesis of the New Testament," in Robinson, ed., *Beginnings of Dialectic Theology*, 1:242.

28. Bultmann, *History and Eschatology*, p. 122.

29. Paul Tillich, *The Courage to Be*, p. 190.

30. Paul Sherer, *The Word God Sent* (New York: Harper & Row, 1965), p. 48.

31. Amos Wilder, *Otherworldiness and the New Testament*, p. 48.

32. Amos Wilder, *New Testament Faith for Today*, p. 35.

33. Ibid., p. 87.

34. Ibid.

35. Wilder, *Otherworldiness*, pp. 99–100.

36. Paul Minear, *Eyes of Faith*, p. 15.

37. Ibid., p. 25.

38. Paul Minear, "Christian Eschatology and Historical Methodology," in Walter Ellester, ed., *Neutestamentliche Studien für Rudolf Bultmann* (Berlin: A. Töpelmann, 1954), p. 20.

39. Paul Minear, *The Kingdom and the Power*, p. 122.

40. Bultmann, *Jesus Christ and Mythology*, p. 55.

41. Ibid.

42. Schubert M. Ogden, *Christ without Myth*, p. 69.

43. Bultmann, "New Testament and Mythology," p. 25.

44. Ibid., p. 27.

45. Bultmann, *Theology of the New Testament*, 1:191.

Chapter 4

1. Karl Barth, "Foreword to the First Edition, *Epistle to the Romans*," in James M. Robinson, ed., *The Beginnings of Dialectic Theology*, (Richmond: John Knox Press, 1968) 1:61.

2. Emil Brunner, "An Up-to-Date, Unmodern Paraphrase," in Robinson, ed., *Beginnings of Dialectic Theology*, 1:64.

3. Karl Barth, *How I Changed My Mind*, ed. John D. Godsey (Richmond: John Knox Press, 1966), p. 43.

4. Rudolf Bultmann, "Karl Barth's *Epistle to the Romans* in Its Second Edition," in Robinson, ed., *Beginnings of Dialectic Theology*, 1:111.

5. Ibid., p. 108.

6. Cited by Schubert M. Ogden, "The Debate on 'Demythologizing,'" *Journal of Bible and Religion* 27 (1959):21.

7. Bultmann, "Autobiographical Reflections," p. 288.

8. Rudolf Bultmann, "Concerning the Hidden and Revealed God," in *Existence and Faith*, pp. 29, 30.

9. Rudolf Bultmann, "Humanism and Christianity," in *Essays*, p. 153.

10. Rudolf Bultmann, "Christ the End of the Law," in *Essays*, pp. 46–47.

11. Rudolf Bultmann, "The Question of Natural Revelation," in *Essays*, p. 100.

12. Rudolf Bultmann, "The Problem of 'Natural Theology,'" in Funk, ed., *Faith and Understanding*, 1:318.

13. Bultmann, "The Question of Natural Revelation," p. 109.

14. Rudolf Bultmann, "The Concept of the Word of God in the New Testament," in *Faith and Understanding*, 1:306.

15. Ibid.

16. Bultmann, "New Testament and Mythology," in Bartsch, ed., *Kerygma and Myth*, 1:41.

17. Rudolf Bultmann, *This World and the Beyond: Marburg Sermons*, trans. H. Knight (New York: Charles Scribner's Sons, 1960), p. 221.

18. Rudolf Bultmann, "Bultmann Replies to His Critics," in Bartsch, ed., *Kerygma and Myth*, 1:209.

19. Bultmann, *Jesus Christ and Mythology*, p. 78.

20. Ibid., p. 82.

21. Rudolf Bultmann, "The Christology of the New Testament," in *Faith and Understanding*, 1:278.

22. Bultmann, *Theology of the New Testament*, 1:191.

23. Ibid., 302.

24. Rudolf Bultmann, "The Problem of a Theological Exegesis," in Robinson, ed., *Beginnings of Dialectic Theology*, 1:254.

25. Bultmann, *Jesus Christ and Mythology*, p. 71.

26. Ibid., p. 53.

27. Rudolf Bultmann, "The Concept of Revelation in the New Testament," in *Existence and Faith,* p. 77.

28. Bultmann, *Theology of the New Testament*, 1:314–23.

29. Rudolf Bultmann, *Jesus and the Word*, p. 94.

30. Bultmann, *Jesus Christ and Mythology*, p. 31.

31. Langdon Gilkey, "Neo-Orthodoxy," in Halverson and Cohen, eds., *Handbook of Christian Theology*, p. 260.

32. E. A. Burtt, "Some Questions about Niebuhr's Theology," in Charles W. Kegley and Robert W. Bretall, eds., *Reinhold Niebuhr: His Religious, Social and Political Thought* (New York: Macmillan, 1956), pp. 357–58.

33. Reinhold Niebuhr, *Faith and History*, p. 137.

34. Brevard Childs, *Biblical Theology in Crisis* (Philadelphia: Westminster Press, 1970), p. 17.

35. Robert McAfee Brown, *The Bible Speaks to You* (Philadelphia: Westminster Press, 1955), p. 15.

36. Bernhard W. Anderson, *Rediscovering the Bible*, p. 37.

37. G. Ernest Wright, *God Who Acts*, p. 33.

38. Floyd V. Filson, *Jesus Christ the Risen Lord*, p. 13.

39. Ethelbert Stauffer, *New Testament Theology*, p. 87.

40. Ibid., p. 21.

41. Rudolf Bultmann, "The Question of 'Dialectic' Theology," 1:273.

Chapter 5

1. John Knox, *Christ the Lord: The Meaning of Jesus in the Early Church* (Chicago: Willett, Clark and Co., 1945), p. 69.

2. John Knox, *Jesus Lord and Christ: A Triology Comprising The Man Christ Jesus, Christ the Lord, On the Meaning of Christ* (New York: Harper & Bros., 1958), p. 193.

3. Wilhelm Herrmann, "Gottes Offenbarung an Uns," in Peter

Fischer-Appelt, ed., *Schriften zur Grundlegung der Theologie* (Munich: Chr. Kaiser, 1967), 2:150.

4. Wilhelm Herrmann, *The Communion of the Christian with God: A Discussion of Agreement with the View of Luther*, trans. J. S. Stanyon (London: Williams and Norgate, 1895), p. 223.

5. Rudolf Bultmann, "The Question of 'Dialectic' Theology," 1:259.

6. Bultmann, *Jesus Christ and Mythology*, p. 55.

7. Bultmann, "New Testament and Mythology," 1:25.

8. Bultmann, *Jesus Christ and Mythology*, p. 57.

9. Bultmann, "On the Question of Christology," in Funk, ed., *Faith and Understanding*, 1:132.

10. Karl Jaspers and Rudolf Bultmann, *Myth and Christianity: An Inquiry into the Possibility of Religion without Myth*, trans. N. Guterman (New York: Noonday Press, 1958), p. 49.

11. Rudolf Bultmann, "The Significance of Jewish Old Testament Tradition for the Christian West," in *Essays*, p. 271.

12. Bultmann, "New Testament and Mythology," p. 41.

13. Rudolf Bultmann, "Faith as Venture," in *Existence and Faith*, p. 56.

14. Rudolf Bultmann, "Paul," in *Existence and Faith*, p. 141.

15. Bultmann, *Jesus Christ and Mythology*, p. 18.

16. Bultmann, "New Testament and Mythology," 1:10, n. 2.

17. Bultmann, *Jesus Christ and Mythology*, p. 19.

18. Bultmann, "New Testament and Mythology," 1:10.

19. Bultmann, *Jesus Christ and Mythology*, p. 19.

20. Ibid., p. 34.

21. Bultmann, "New Testament and Mythology," 1:11.

22. Jaspers and Bultmann, *Myth and Christianity*, p. 59.

23. Bultmann, *Jesus Christ and Mythology*, p. 18.

24. Ibid.

25. Erich Dinkler, *Journal of Religion* 32 (1952):87 ff.

26. Rudolf Bultmann, "The Question of Wonder," in *Faith and Understanding*, 1:249.

27. Bultmann, *Jesus Christ and Mythology*, p. 85.

28. Bernd Jaspert, ed., *Karl Barth—Rudolf Bultmann: Briefwechsel, 1922–1966* (Zurich: Theologisches Verlag, 1971), p. 183.

29. Rudolf Bultmann, "Bultmann Replies to His Critics," 1:210–11.

30. Bultmann, *Jesus Christ and Mythology*, p. 62.

31. Ibid., p. 80.

32. Karl Barth, "Rudolf Bultmann—An Attempt to Understand Him," in Hans-Werner Bartsch, ed., *Kerygma and Myth: A Theological Debate*, trans. R. H. Fuller, vol. 2 (London: S.P.C.K., 1962), p. 121.

Chapter 6

1. Rudolf Bultmann, *Jesus and the Word*, trans. L. P. Smith and E. H. Lantero (New York: Charles Scribner's Sons, 1958), p. 3.

2. Bultmann, *History and Eschatology*, p. 17.

3. Rudolf Bultmann, "Is Exegesis without Presuppositions Possible?" in *Existence and Faith*, p. 291.

4. Heinrich Ott, *Die Frage nach dem historischen Jesus und die Ontologie der Geschichte*, Theologische Studien, vol. 62 (Zurich: EVZ-Verlag, 1960), p. 11.

5. Bultmann, *History and Eschatology*, p. 122.

6. Herman Ridderbos, *Bultmann*, trans. D. H. Freeman (Philadelphia: Presbyterian and Reformed Publishing Co., 1960), p. 38.

7. Schubert M. Ogden, *Christ without Myth.*

8. Rudolf Bultmann, *Journal of Religion* 42 (1962):226.

9. Langdon Gilkey, "Cosmology, Ontology, and the Travail of Biblical Language," *Journal of Religion* 41 (1961) :194.

10. Van A. Harvey, *The Historian and the Believer*, p. 143.

11. Harald Riesenfeld, "The Mythological Background of New Testament Christology," in W. D. Davies and D. Daube, eds., *The Background of the New Testament and Its Eschatology*, (Cambridge: University Press, 1956), p. 81.

12. Robin Scroggs, *The Last Adam: A Study in Pauline Anthropology* (Philadelphia: Fortress Press, 1966), p. xxiii.

13. Carston Colpe, "New Testament and Gnostic Christology," in Jacob Neusner, ed., *Religions in Antiquity—Essays in Memory of Erwin Ramsdell Goodenough* (Leiden: E. J. Brille, 1968), p. 235.

14. Edwin Yamauchi, *Pre-Christian Gnosticism: A Survey of the*

Proposed Evidences (Grand Rapids: Wm. B. Eerdmans, 1973), p. 165.

15. Rudolf Schnackenburg, "Von der Formgeschichte zur Entmythologisierung des Neuen Testaments—Zur Theologie Rudolf Bultmanns," in Hans Werner Bartsch, ed., *Kerygma und Mythos,* (Hamburg-Volksdorf: Herbert Reich, 1955), pp. 90–91.

16. Heinz Schürmann, "Die vorösterlichen Anfänge der Logientradition—Versuch eines formgeschichtlichen Zugangs zum Leben Jesu," in *Traditionsgeschichtliche Untersuchungen zu den synoptischen Evangelien* (Dusseldorf: Patmos-Verlag, 1968), pp. 51 ff.

17. Willi Marxsen, *Mark the Evangelist,* p. 23.

18. Humphrey Palmer, *The Logic of Gospel Criticism* (New York: St. Martin's Press, 1968), p. 183.

19. Norman Perrin, *What Is Redaction Criticism?* (Philadelphia: Fortress Press, 1969), p. 74.

20. Morton Scott Enslin, *The Prophet from Nazareth* (New York, Toronto, London: McGraw-Hill, 1961), p. 14.

21. Joachim Jeremias, *The Problem of the Historical Jesus,* p. 12.

22. N. A. Dahl, "The Problem of the Historical Jesus," in Carl E. Braaten and Roy A. Harrisville, eds., *Kerygma and History—A Symposium on the Theology of Rudolf Bultmann* (New York: Abingdon Press, 1962), p. 158.

23. Jeremias, "The Problem of the Historical Jesus," p. 21.

24. Otto Betz, *What do we know about Jesus?* (London: SCM Press, 1968), p. 13.

25. Ernst Käsemann, *The Problem of the Historical Jesus,* in *Essays on New Testament Themes,* p. 25.

26. Ibid.

27. James M. Robinson, *A New Quest of the Historical Jesus,* p. 92.

28. Günther Bornkamm, "Myth and Gospel: A Discussion of the Problem of Demythologizing the New Testament Message," in Braaten and Harrisville, eds., *Kerygma and History,* p. 24.

29. Heinz Zahrnt, *The Historical Jesus,* trans. J. S. Bowden (New York and Evanston: Harper & Row, 1963), p. 135.

30. Leander Keck, *A Future for the Historical Jesus: The Place of Jesus in Preaching and Theology* (Nashville: Abingdon Press, 1971), p. 35.

31. Ibid., p. 48.

32. Harvey, *Historian and Believer*, pp. 253 ff.

33. Ibid., pp. 266 ff.

34. F. H. Heinemann, *Existentialism and the Modern Predicament*, 2d ed. (New York: Harper & Bros., 1954), p. 151.

35. Ibid., p. 174.

36. Frederick Sontag, *The Future of Theology: A Philosophical Basis for Contemporary Protestant Thought* (Philadelphia: Westminster Press, 1969), p. 59.

37. Bultmann, *Theology of the New Testament*, 1:191.

38. Ogden, *Christ without Myth*, p. 148.

39. Sontag, *Future of Theology*, p. 71.

40. Bultmann, "Bultmann Replies to His Critics," in Bartsch, ed., *Kerygma and Myth*, 1:211.

41. Ibid.

42. John Macquarrie, *Existentialism* (Philadelphia: Westminster Press, 1972), p. 220.

43. Bultmann, *History and Eschatology*, p. 96.

44. Thomas Oden, *Radical Obedience: The Ethics of Rudolf Bultmann* (Philadelphia: Westminster Press, 1964), p. 117.

45. Dorothee Soelle, *Political Theology*, trans. J. Shelley (Philadelphia: Fortress Press, 1974), p. 48.

46. William Hordern, "Neo-Orthodoxy or Post-Neo-Orthodoxy," *Religion in Life* 30 (1960–61):554.

47. Langdon Gilkey, *Naming the Whirlwind*, p. 22.

48. Hermann Timm, *Theorie und Praxis in der Theologie Albrecht Ritschls und Wilhelm Herrmanns* (Gutersloh: Gerd Mohn, 1967), p. 14.

49. Hans-Joachim Kraus, *Die Biblische Theologie: Ihre Geschichte und Problematik* (Neukirchen-Vluyn: Neukirchener Verlag, 1970), p. 331.

50. John Cobb, *A Christian Natural Theology*, p. 243.

51. Ulrich Mauser, *Gottesbild und Menschwerdung*, p. 190.

52. Ronald W. Hepburn, "Demythologizing and the Problem of Validity," in *New Essays in Philosophical Theology* (London: SCM Press, 1955), p. 228.

53. H. Richard Niebuhr, "Reformation: Continuing Imperative," *Christian Century* 77 (1960) :250.

54. G. Ernest Wright, *The Old Testament and Theology* (New York, Evanston, and London: Harper & Row, 1969), p. 9.

55. Ernst Käsemann, "The Beginnings of Christian Theology," in *New Testament Questions*, p. 96.

56. Ibid., p. 102.

57. Wolfhart Pannenberg, *Jesus, God and Man*, p. 69.

58. Jürgen Moltmann, *Theology of Hope*, p. 93.

59. Käsemann, " 'The Righteousness of God' in Paul," in *New Testament Questions*, p. 180.

60. Robert T. Voelkel, *The Shape of the Theological Task* (Philadelphia: Westminster Press, 1968), p. 103.

61. James M. Robinson, "Hermeneutic Since Barth," in James M. Robinson and John B. Cobb, Jr., eds., *The New Hermeneutic*, New Frontiers in Theology, vol. 2 (New York: Harper & Row, 1964), p. 67.

62. Ernst Fuchs, "The Essence of the 'Language-Event' and Christology," in *Studies of the Historical Jesus*, p. 223.

63. Robinson, "Hermeneutic Since Barth," p. 67.

64. Langdon Gilkey, "Secularism's Impact on Contemporary Theology," *Christianity and Crisis* 25 (1965–66) :66.

Selected Bibliography

Cited here are some representative works of major figures discussed in the text.

Anderson, Bernhard W. *Rediscovering the Bible.* New York: Association Press, 1951.

Barr, James. *The Semantics of Biblical Language.* Oxford: University Press, 1961.

Barth, Karl. *The Epistle to the Romans.* Translated by E. C. Hoskyns. London New York, and Toronto: Oxford University Press, 1933.

Berdyaev, Nicholas. *The Destiny of Man.* Translated by N. Duddington. London: Geoffrey Bles, 1954.

————. *The Meaning of History.* Translated by G. Reavey. London: Geoffrey Bles, 1936.

Bornkamm, Günther. *Jesus of Nazareth.* Translated by I. and F. McLuskey. New York: Harper & Bros., 1960.

Bousset, Wilhelm. *The Faith of a Modern Protestant.* Translated by F. B. Low. New York: Charles Scribner's Sons, 1909.

————. *Kyrios Christos.* Translated by J. E. Steely. Nashville: Abingdon Press, 1970.

Brunner, Emil. *Revelation and Reason.* Translated by O. Wyon. Philadelphia: Westminster Press, 1946.

Buber, Martin. *I and Thou*. Translated by R. G. Smith. 2d ed. New York: Charles Scribner's Sons, 1958.

Bultmann, Rudolf. *Essays—Philosophical and Theological*. Translated by J. C. G. Greig. New York: Macmillan, 1955.

———. *Existence and Faith: Shorter Writings of Rudolf Bultmann*. Translated by Schubert M. Ogden. New York: Meridian Books, 1960.

———. *Faith and Understanding*. Vol. 1. Edited by R. W. Funk. Translated by L. P. Smith. New York: Harper & Row, 1969.

———. *History and Eschatology*. New York: Harper & Row, Harper Torchbooks, 1962.

———. *The History of the Synoptic Tradition*. Translated by J. Marsh. New York: Harper & Row, 1963.

———. *Jesus Christ and Mythology*. New York: Charles Scribner's Sons, 1958.

———. *Jesus and the Word*. Translated by L. P. Smith and E. H. Lantero. New York: Charles Scribner's Sons, 1958.

———. *Primitive Christianity in Its Contemporary Setting*. Translated by R. H. Fuller. New York: Meridian Books, 1957.

———. *Theology of the New Testament*. Translated by K. Grobel. 2 vols. New York: Charles Scribner's Sons, 1951, 1955.

Burkitt, F. C. *The Church and Gnosis*. Cambridge: University Press, 1932.

Burrows, Millar. *An Outline of Biblical Theology*. Philadelphia: Westminster Press, 1946.

Cadbury, Henry J. *The Peril of Modernizing Jesus*. New York: Macmillan, 1937.

Case, Shirley Jackson. *The Evolution of Early Christianity*. Chicago: University of Chicago Press, 1914.

———. *The Social Origins of Christianity*. Chicago: University of Chicago Press, 1923.

Cobb, John. *A Christian Natural Theology: Based on the Thought of Alfred North Whitehead*. Philadelphia: Westminster Press, 1965.

Colpe, Carsten. *Die religionsgeschichtliche Schule: Darstellung und Kritik ihres Bildes vom gnostischen Erlösermythus*. Göttingen: Vandenhoeck und Ruprecht, 1961.

Conzelmann, Hans. *An Outline of the Theology of the New Testament*.

Translated by J. Bowden. New York and Evanston: Harper & Row, 1969.

———. *The Theology of St. Luke.* Translated by G. Buswell. New York: Harper & Bros., 1960.

Cullmann, Oscar. *Christ and Time: The Primitive Christian Conception of Time and History.* 3rd ed. Translated by F. V. Filson. London: SCM Press, 1962.

———. *Salvation in History.* Translated by S. G. Sowers. London: SCM Press, 1967.

Davies, W. D. *Paul and Rabbinic Judaism.* London: S.P.C.K., 1948.

Dibelius, Martin. *From Tradition to Gospel.* Translated by B. L. Woolf. New York: Charles Scribner's Sons, 1935.

Dinkler, Erich. *Signum Crucis: Aufsätze zum Neuen Testament und zur Christlichen Archäologie.* Tübingen: J. C. B. Mohr, 1967.

Dodd, C. H. *The Apostolic Preaching.* New York: Harper & Bros., 1960.

———. *The Interpretation of the Fourth Gospel.* Cambridge: University Press, 1954.

———. *The Parables of the Kingdom.* Rev. ed. New York: Charles Scribner's Sons, 1961.

Easton, Burton Scott. *The Gospel before the Gospels.* New York: Charles Scribner's Sons, 1928.

Ebeling, Gerhard. *Word and Faith.* Translated by J. W. Leitch. Philadelphia: Fortress Press, 1963.

Farmer, William R. *The Synoptic Problem.* New York: Macmillan, 1964.

Fashcher, Erich. *Die formgeschichtliche Methode.* Giessen: Alfred Töpelmann, 1924.

Filson, Floyd V. *Jesus Christ the Risen Lord.* New York: Abingdon Press, 1956.

———. *One Lord, One Faith.* Philadelphia: Westminster Press, 1943.

Fuchs, Ernst. *Hermeneutik.* 2d ed. Bad Cannstatt: R. Müllerschön, 1958.

———. *Studies of the Historical Jesus.* Translated by A. Scobie. Studies in Biblical Theology, vol. 42. Naperville, Ill.: Alec R. Allenson, 1964.

Gerhardsson, Birger. *Memory and Manuscript: Oral Tradition and*

Written Transmission in Rabbinic Judaism and Early Christianity. Translated by E. J. Sharpe. Lund: C. W. K. Gleerup, 1961.

Gilkey, Langdon. *Naming the Whirlwind: The Renewal of God-Language.* Indianapolis: Bobbs-Merrill, 1969.

Goodenough, Erwin R. *Jewish Symbols in the Greco-Roman Period.* 12 vols. Bollingen Series 37. New York: Pantheon Books, 1953–1965.

———. *By Light, Light: The Mystic Gospel of Hellenistic Judaism.* New Haven: Yale University, 1935.

Grant, Frederick C. *An Introduction to New Testament Thought.* New York: Abingdon-Cokesbury, 1950.

———. *The Gospels: Their Origin and Their Growth.* New York: Harper & Bros., 1957.

Gunkel, Hermann. *Legends of Genesis.* Translated by W. H. Carruth. Chicago: Open Court, 1901.

———. *The Psalms: A Form-Critical Introduction.* Translated by T. M. Horner. Biblical Series, vol. 19. Philadelphia: Fortress Press, 1967.

Güttgemanns, Erhardt, *Offene Fragen zur Formgeschichte des Evangeliums.* Munich: Chr. Kaiser, 1970.

Harnack, Adolf. *What Is Christianity.* Translated by Thomas B. Saunders. New York: Harper & Bros., 1957.

Hartshorne, Charles. *The Divine Relativity: A Social Conception of God.* New Haven: Yale University, 1948.

———. *Man's Vision of God.* Chicago: Willett, Clark and Co., 1941.

Harvey, Van A. *The Historian and the Believer: The Morality of Historical Knowledge and Christian Belief.* New York: Macmillan, 1966.

Hatch, Edwin. *The Influence of Greek Ideas on Christianity.* New York: Harper & Row, 1957.

Heidegger, Martin. *Being and Time.* Translated by J. Macquarrie and E. Robinson. New York: Harper & Bros., 1962.

Herrmann, Wilhelm. *The Communion of the Christian with God.* Edited by Robert T. Voelkel. Philadelphia: Fortress Press, 1971.

———. *Schriften zur Grundlegung der Theologie.* Edited by P. Fischer-Appelt. Munich: Chr. Kaiser, 1967.

Hoskyns, Edwyn, and Davey, Noel. *The Riddle of the New Testament.* 3d ed. London: Faber and Faber, 1947.

Hoskyns, Edwyn Clement. *The Fourth Gospel,* Edited by F. N. Davey. London: Faber and Faber, 1947.

Jeremias, Joachim. *The Central Message of the New Testament.* New York: Charles Scribner's Sons, 1965.

———. *The Parables of Jesus.* Translated by S. H. Hooke. Rev. ed. New York: Charles Scribner's Sons, 1963.

———. *The Problem of the Historical Jesus.* Translated by N. Perrin. Biblical Series, vol. 13. Philadelphia: Fortress Press, 1964.

Jüngel, Eberhard. *Paulus und Jesus.* Tübingen: J. C. B. Mohr, 1962.

Kähler, Martin. *The So-Called Historical Jesus and the Historic Biblical Christ.* Translated by C. E. Braaten. Philadelphia: Fortress Press, 1964.

Käsemann, Ernst. *Essays on New Testament Themes.* Translated by W. J. Montague. Studies in Biblical Theology, vol. 41. London: SCM Press, 1964.

———. *New Testament Questions of Today.* Translated by W. J. Montague. Philadelphia: Fortress Press, 1969.

———. *Perspectives on Paul.* Translated by M. Kohl. Philadephia: Fortress Press, 1971.

Kaufman, Gordon D. *Systematic Theology: A Historicist Perspective.* New York: Charles Scribner's Sons, 1968.

Kennedy, H. A. A. *St. Paul and the Mystery Religions.* London: Hodder and Stoughton, 1913.

Klein, Günter. *Rekonstruktion und Interpretation—Gesammelte Aufsätze zum Neuen Testament.* Munich: Chr. Kaiser, 1969.

Knox, John. *The Church and the Reality of Christ.* New York: Harper & Row, 1962.

———. *Criticism and Faith.* New York: Abingdon Press, 1952.

———. *Jesus Lord and Christ: A Triology Comprising The Man Christ Jesus, Christ the Lord, On the Meaning of Christ.* New York: Harper & Bros., 1958.

Kraeling, Carl H. *Anthropos and Son of Man: A Study of the Religious Syncretism of the Hellenistic Orient.* New York: Columbia University, 1927.

Lightfoot, R. H. *History and Interpretation in the Gospels*. New York and London: Harper & Bros., 1934.

Machen, J. Gresham. *The Virgin Birth of Jesus*. New York and London: Macmillan, 1921.

Marcel, Gabriel. *Men Against Humanity*. Translated by G. S. Fraser. London: Harvill Press, 1952.

———. *The Mystery of Being: II. Faith and Reality*. Translated by R. Hague. Chicago: Henry Regnery, 1951.

Marxsen, Willi. *The Beginnings of Christology: A Study in Its Problems*. Translated by P. J. Achtemeier. Philadelphia: Fortress Press, 1969.

———. *Mark the Evangelist: Studies on the Redaction History of the Gospel*. Translated by J. Boyce, D. Juel, W. Poehlmann and R. A. Harrisville. Nashville: Abingdon Press, 1969.

Mauser, Ulrich. *Gottesbild und Menschwerdung: Eine Untersuchung zur Einheit der Alten und Neuen Testaments*. Tübingen: J. C. B. Mohr, 1971.

Minear, Paul S. *Eyes of Faith: A Study in the Biblical Point of View*. Philadelphia: Westminster Press, 1946.

———. *I Saw a New Earth: An Introduction to the Visions of the Apocalypse*. Washington: Corpus Books, 1968.

———. *The Kingdom and the Power: An Exposition of the New Testament Gospel*. Philadelphia: Westminster Press, 1946.

Moltmann, Jürgen. *Theology of Hope*. Translated by J. W. Leitch. New York: Harper & Row, 1967.

Müller, Christian. *Gottes Gerechtigkeit und Gottes Volk: Eine Untersuchung zu Römer 9–11*. Göttingen: Vandenhoeck und Ruprecht, 1964.

Niebuhr, H. Richard. *The Meaning of Revelation*. New York: Macmillan, 1946.

Niebuhr, Reinhold. *Faith and History*. New York: Charles Scribner's Sons, 1949.

———. *The Nature and Destiny of Man*. New York: Charles Scribner's Sons, 1945.

Nock, Arthur Darby. *Early Gentile Christianity and Its Hellenistic Background*. New York: Harper & Row, 1964.

Ogden, Schubert. *Christ without Myth: A Study Based on the The-

ology of Rudolf Bultmann. New York, Evanston, and London: Harper & Row, 1961.

Palmer, Humphrey. *The Logic of Gospel Criticism.* New York: St. Martin's Press, 1968.

Pannenberg, Wolfhart. *Jesus: God and Man.* Translated by L. L. Wilkins and D. A. Priebe. Philadelphia: Westminster Press, 1968.

Reitzenstein, Richard. *Die Hellenistischen Mysterienreligionen.* 3d ed. Stuttgart: B. G. Teubner, 1956.

Richardson, Alan. *An Introduction to the Theology of the New Testament.* New York: Harper & Bros., 1958.

Riesenfeld, Harald. *The Gospel Tradition.* Translated by E. M. Rowley and R. A. Kraft. Philadelphia: Fortress Press, 1970.

Robinson, James M. *A New Quest of the Historical Jesus.* Studies in Biblical Theology, vol. 25. London: SCM Press, 1959.

Robinson, John A. T. *Honest to God.* Philadelphia: Westminster Press, 1963.

Sanders, E. P. *The Tendencies of the Synoptic Tradition.* Cambridge: University Press, 1969.

Schenke, Hans-Martin. *Der Gott 'Mensch' in der Gnosis.* Göttingen: Vandenhoeck and Ruprecht, 1962.

Schmidt, Karl Ludwig. *Der Rahmen der Geschichte Jesu.* Berlin: Trowitzsch und Sohn, 1919.

Schweitzer, Albert. *The Quest of the Historical Jesus: A Critical Study of Its Progress from Reimarus to Wrede.* Translated by W. Montgomery. New York: Macmillan, 1957.

Scott, Ernest Findlay. *The Validity of the Gospel Record.* New York: Charles Scribner's Sons, 1938.

Stauffer, Ethelbert. *New Testament Theology.* Translated by J. Marsh. New York: Macmillan, 1955.

Stuhlmacher, Peter. *Gerechtigkeit Gottes bei Paulus.* Göttingen: Vandenhoeck und Ruprecht, 1965.

Taylor, Vincent. *The Formation of the Gospel Tradition.* London: Macmillan, 1933.

Tillich, Paul. *The Courage to Be.* New Haven: Yale University, 1952.

Weiss, Johannes. *Jesus' Proclamation of the Kingdom of God.* Translated by H. R. Hiers and D. L. Holland. Philadelphia: Fortress Press, 1971.

Wilder, Amos. *New Testament Faith for Today*. New York: Harper & Bros., 1955.

————. *Otherworldliness and the New Testament*. New York: Harper & Bros., 1954.

Wrede, William. *The Messianic Secret*. Translated by J. C. G. Greig. Cambridge: J. Clarke, 1971.

Wright, G. Ernest. *God Who Acts: Biblical Theology as Recital*. Studies in Biblical Theology, vol. 8. London: SCM Press, 1956.

Index of Names